Welche Gordon

Jesse James and his Band of Notorious Outlaws

Welche Gordon

Jesse James and his Band of Notorious Outlaws

ISBN/EAN: 9783337337513

Printed in Europe, USA, Canada, Australia, Japan

Cover: Foto ©Thomas Meinert / pixelio.de

More available books at **www.hansebooks.com**

The Pinkerton Detective Series.

LAIRD & LEE, Publishers,

203-205 JACKSON ST. CHICAGO, ILL.

JESSE JAMES.

JESSE JAMES

And His Band of Notorious Outlaws

BY

WELCHE GORDON

COPYRIGHT 1890 BY LAIRD & LEE

ALL RIGHTS RESERVED

———

The PINKERTON DETECTIVE SERIES. Issued Monthly
By Subscription $3.00 per annum. No. 42 August 1890.
Entered at Chicago Postoffice as second class matter.

———

CHICAGO
LAIRD & LEE PUBLISHERS
1891

CHAPTER I

Outlaws, bandits, pirates and highwaymen have been favorite subjects of the novelist and story-tellers, since the art of writing and the science of narratory have existed. The subjects were in a lively state of activity ages before the stylus of the Egyptian, and the wax tablets of the Greeks were ever invented. The inspired pen of Moses wrote of Cain, the first outlaw, the original murderer. The historians of the ancient Hebrews immortalized the Ishmaelites, the wonders of the desert, whose hands were against the hands of the rest of mankind.

St. Paul relates his adventures with pirates and robbers, and Josephus tells of the raids of armed and organized bandits.

Robin Hood and his merry men have been the inspiration of the minstrels and writers of medieval times. Dick Turpin, the gallant, bold king of the road, the dashing highwayman, has furnished material for innumerable tales, and his exploits will live as long as mankind exists.

Who has not read of "Paul Clifford," that romantic, elegant, dashing gentleman, who would calmly and politely rob a coach and four while on his way to pay a surreptitious call upon his fond sweetheart.

Captain Kidd, the pirate bold, has kept many innocent readers of his adventures awake until the grey dawn peeped between the jealous curtains, and Byron lent his genius in singing of that hand-some buccaneer, Don Juan. And now an humble and impecunious scribbler wets his clumsy pen with thick ink to give a gaping and yawning world the history of one who, disdaining the glamour which envelopes the romantic scoundrels of "ye olden days," stands the superior of all in audacity and rashness, courage and nerve, brutality and hellishness—Jesse James.

How can one begin the tale of this terrible man?

What language can furnish the vocabulary which contains enough lurid words, wild synonyms, en-sanguinary adjectives, and murderous verbs, to do justice to this horrible monster; this insatiable vampire who has drank enough blood to print in red, an entire edition of this narrative?

Dead though he be, incapable of harming even a child; though he was at last overtaken by a tardy retribution, his memory alone still causes the strong man to look askance as he passes along the lonely Missouri roads which once echoed with the hoofbeats of Jesse James' wild horses, and makes the brave heart tremble at the sudden shadow cast by the waving tree limbs which once served to shelter this messenger of death.

That ancient, and weather beaten truism, "Facts are stranger than fiction" acquires additional vigor, and renewed youth, when applied to the life and adventures of Jesse James. No novelist in his wildest flights of fancy, no writer urged on by the maddest vagaries of a heated imagination, no pen possessed of inventive genius short of Satanic, could conjure up such a character, trace so wild a life, or create such dramatic tableaux.

The plain unvarnished facts which will relate to you the career, adventures, escapades, and death of this Jesse James, will seem too strange, and extravagant to be true, but the compiler of this history is not gifted with the genius of imagery, and must, forsooth, write facts, facts, facts, hard pitiless, terrible facts, and then, he will have told but a part.

CHAPTER II

JESSE AND FRANK JAMES

THE YOUTHFUL NIMRODS—BECOMING CRACK SHOTS
QUANTRELL'S SAD STORY—THE DEATH OATH—
FRANK JAMES BECOMES A GUERILLA—A
CRUEL OUTRAGE—JESSE JOINS
QUANTRELL

To mention Jesse James, is to speak of his brother, Frank. Kentucky, the "Bloody Ground" of Daniel Boone and early pioneer days, must share with Missouri, the "Bloodier Ground" of later days, the memorable honor of calling the James boys their sons.

It was in the year of 1845, that Frank James, the elder of the brothers, entered this world in Scott County, Kentucky. His father, by the cruel satire of events, was a Baptist clergyman.

Four years later Jesse was born into the world in Clay county, Missouri; the family having moved to that locality shortly after the birth of Frank.

It was a ghastly joke of circumstances that surrounded these two lads with the pious atmosphere of a minister's family, for their father was a good, sincere expounder of the divine truths, and labored incessantly in his new vineyard.

Providence was kind to him ever, for, becoming

enthused with the fever of '49, the reverend gentleman gave up his pastorate, and set his face to the sun which set over the gold fields of California. He left his family in Missouri, traveled over the plains to the Golden State, and never returned, for contracting a mortal disease, he died far away from his home and wife, and was thus spared the anguish which would surely have been his had he lived to witness the deeds which rang through the entire country, coupled with his family name.

The mother, Mrs. James was made of different material than her husband, and, of the two, she was certainly the most masculine. Although left alone, comparatively speaking, in the world, she put on the harness, and brought up her family, unaided and alone, until seven years had past, when she again became a bride, and left the church on the arm of her second husband, Dr. Reuben Samuels.

Frank and Jesse had grown into strong lusty lads, the terrors of their companions. Quick to resent a fancied or real affront, eager to pick up a quarrel upon the slighest provocation, and never hesitating to mete out the fullest punishment their ungracious minds could invent, they were dreaded by the neighbors, and feared by everybody.

Dr. Samuels seems to have been attached to them for, among other presents, he gave them each a double barreled shot gun. In a short time both lads became veritable Nimrods, and, having already acquired a knowledge of woodcraft which filled their young minds with a strong desire to know more, they spent all their time with the favorite guns, and kept the family larder supplied with game.

Before long, each boy was the proud possessor of a revolver, and they became as expert with their pistols as they were with their shot guns.

Fired with the ambition to excel all others in the use of this universal fire arm, they practised incessantly, thus laying the foundation of that wonderful accuracy and marksmanship which distinguished them in the stirring events so soon to follow.

The civil war had begun, and Quantrell the famous guerilla chief was ranging western Missouri with his wild band of devoted followers. This noted bandit was a creature of circumstances. He became what he was through one single cruel wrong. The unexpected events of a single hour turned him from the peaceful pursuits of a law-abiding citizen into a human tiger, a monster of blood and crime.

The story is a sad one, for it is the tale of a crime which begat a greater crime, of a ruined life, a murderous existence and a damned soul. ·

Charles William Quantrell, a native of Maryland, and afterwards a good citizen of Cleveland, was a man of education and refined tastes. He was but twenty years of age when the terrible cross-road of his life was reached. With his elder brother, who was more than a brother to him, and whom he loved and respected as a father, he was en route to the gold fields of California. They had with them a negro servant and had proceeded, in their emigrant prairie-schooner, as far as Kansas.

One night, when camped on the banks of the Cottonwood River, enjoying the beautiful cool of the evening air, smoking their pipes and planning for the future, they were suddenly startled by the appearance of thirty men on horse-back, whom they recognized as Jay-hawkers.

These banditti, captained by a man named Lane, were blood-thirsty rascals, who, under the name of Abolitionists, ranged all Kansas, committing the most atrocious crimes, and blood-thirsty acts, robbing and murdering wherever they rode.

The mounted men came toward the quiet camp with the speed of pursued demons, and, without warning, fired a volley into the two brothers.

Riddled by the murderous bullets, the elder brother fell a lifeless corpse, and Charles, struck by a number of the leaden missles, fell across his body, apparently a dead man. Plunder followed the murder, and, in a few minutes, the tent, wagon, negro, and horses, with all the gold seeker's paraphanalia was moving across the plain surrounded by the devilish murderers.

Young Quantrell lay senseless and bleeding until the next morning, and for two days, he prayed for

death between his delirious ravings. The buzzards
and coyotes hovered near him, grim forebodings of
death, and the pitiless sun beat upon his bursting
head, filling the hot brain with all the disordered
fancies of a fevered mind. But his strong constitution pulled him through, and he lived, lived
to kneel beside the corpse of his dead brother and
swear to be avenged. Wept and cursed, prayed
and raved, but determined to live, live until every
hair on his dead brother's head would be avenged.

In the morning of the third day after the outrage,
an old Shawnee Indian, Golightly Spieback, passed
by and found the grief-stricken lad.

Tenderly his skillful fingers bound up the wounds,
deftly and quickly he prepared meat for the weak
body, and, when the body was nourished and the
wounds bandaged, the old Indian dug a grave and
buried the poor slaughtered brother. To his Indian
home he carried the bereaved Quantrell, and nursed
him back to complete health.

Then the active guerilla life of the famous outlaw
began. Sworn to be revenged, hating with an implacable hatred the very name of Jay-hawkers, merciless and cruel to every member of the order who
fell into his eager hands, considering no torture
too severe, no punishment too barbarous for such
men, he soon became the feared and dreaded foe of
every band of Jay-hawkers in Kansas and Missouri.

The war of the Rebellion added new zest and fury
to the Border warfare, and Quantrell gathered

around him a band of young Missourians who loved
him as their captain, and who followed him wherever
he rode. Such famous bordermen as Todd, Anderson, Gregg, and the Younger brothers acknowledged
him as chieftan and gloried in the dark folds of his
black flag. The tales of their exploits, exaggerat-
ed by repetition, reached the hungry ears of Frank
James and fired his youthful heart with a great ambition. He longed to be enrolled under the "black
flag." His adventuresome spirit urged him to go,
and so, in 1862, mounted on a fleet horse, armed
with a rifle and his beloved revolvers, he rode
to Quantrell.

There is no doubt but that both Dr. Samuels and
his spouse approved of this act. Their sympathies
were all with the south in the conflict, and Quantrell was borne with a great deal of complacency by
the partizans of the Confederates, who made up a
large part of the people of Clay county. Whenever
the guerilla chieftain captured and shot a roving
band of Jayhawkers, or put to flight a company of
Missouri militiamen, the deeds were applauded,
and the little eccentricities in the shape of a few
stolen horses, or a couple of burned barns, were
looked on as playful idiosyncrasies of the lively
bravos.

Mrs. Samuels, especially, was loyal to the south.
Her voice was fearlessly raised in the cause she
espoused, and she openly displayed her hatred to
the blue uniforms of the Yankee soldiers. By vari-

ous means she managed to learn of the movements of the Union troops, and whenever the information was important, she would mount Jesse upon a fleet horse and send him to Quantrell. So open and obnoixous was Mrs. Samuels in her demonstrations of southern love, that the Federal militiamen began to notice it. From mere notice suspicion was aroused. Her house was watched, and it became known that several secret midnight conclaves had been held there.

For some time the militia did not interfere, but at length patience ceased to be a particular virtue, and it was decided to pay the Samuels a visit.

It was in June of 1862 that this little bit of ceremony occurred. A company of Missouri militia marched to Kearney and came to a halt before the Samuels homestead.

In language which was not veiled in diplomatic courtesy, they told the venerable doctor that he and his family were in league with Quantrell and his gang, that his house was used as a secret council chamber for the guerrillas, that his son, Jesse James, was the go-between employed by Quantrell, and that his wife was an obnoxious character who had become as stench to the nostrils of the true believers, and that they were going to make an example of himself and Jesse.

The latter was plowing in a distant field and Mrs. Samuels was in the house, out of sight, but within hearing.

YOUNG JESSE AS A SCOUT.

The doctor listened to the tirade, and then pleaded with them to leave him alone, urging that he was a peaceful farmer who did not care to take any part in the quarrel. To this appeal the militia replied by ribald remarks and coarse jests. Then the rope was produced, and, after pinioning his arms securely, the noose was adjusted around his neck, and he was drawn into the air. Leaving him hanging there, they left in a body for Jesse.

Mrs. Samuels had witnessed the outrage, and, as soon as an intervening grove hid the soldiers from sight, flew to the rescue. With almost superhuman strength, she climbed the tree and cut her husband down. He fell like a dead man, but, after working for some time, she revived him and took him to a place of safety.

In the meantime the gallant troop who counterfeited soldiers, went after Jesse, and found him plowing. Placing a rope around his neck, they threatened to hang him to the nearest tree unless he told them where they could find Quantrell.

But, though only sixteen years of age, Jesse James possessed a lion heart, and he remained stolid and indifferent, preserving a contemptuous silence.

Somewhat awed by the spirit of the boy, they left him alone, after swearing dire vengeance if he undertook any more midnight rides for Quantrell's benefit.

Supposing Dr. Samuels to be quite dead by this time, and in good spirits over the day's sport, they left the farm. Learning, however, that the doughty doctor was still very much alive, and that Jesse continued his night rides, they again appeared before the house, and demanded both men, but they found them absent, no one at home but Mrs. Samuels and her daughter, Susie.

Furious at their ill success, and rendered still more angry at the vixen tongue of Mrs. Samuels, who relished nothing better than a war of vindictive metaphors and vexful phrases, they arrested both the mother and daughter and carried them to the jail at St. Joseph.

Here they were incarcerated for weeks, subjected to all the insults which the ingenuity of the vulgar crowd could invent, but, an implacable hater hersel, Mrs. Samuels gave them as good as they sent, and they were glad to let her go.

With his brother Frank a member of Quantrell's band, his mother and sister prisoners, his stepfather and himself hunted fugitives, Jesse determined to join Frank.

He had again and again begged permission to enter the band, but was considered too young. He was barely sixteen years of age with the smooth face of a girl, but the muscles of an athlete.

Determined however to fight under Quantrell's standard, smarting under the insults he had borne and burning for vengeance, he mounted his horse and sped for the guerilla encampment. He was this time received with open arms and from that time on with his brother Frank, was the boldest, most daring, wildest member of the company.

CHAPTER III

THE RICHFIELD RAID

MURDER OF SESSIONS AND GROFFENSTEIN—A SUCCESS-
FUL RAID—JESSE AS A SCOUT—PLATTSBURG
RAIDED—CAPTAIN RODGERS A CAP-
TIVE—A STRANGE BANQUET—
TERRIBLE CONDITION OF
AFFAIRS

Shortly after the James boys had become members of Quantrell's band the guerilla chief determined to engage more actively in the struggle then
going on between the north and south. Clay, Clinton and Platte counties were in a large degree sym-
pathizers of the sunny south—at least two-thirds of
the population were partizans of the rebel forces.

The war fever raged with growing heat. The
fullest bitterness of the conflict was drank to the
dregs. Families were divided, brothers antagonized
brothers, sons arrayed themselves against their
fathers, and the spirit of the times created feuds
on all sides.

Excitement ran high and the slumbering passion
of the community burst into a flame when the Federal troops entered that section of Missouri, and
took up their quarters in the various towns.

The town of Richfield stood on the northern banks

of the Missouri river, and was selected on account
of its locality and strategic situation, as a Federal
garrison. The company stationed there was but a
small one, composed of thirty-five men, commanded
by a Captain Sessions.

Quantrell was too experienced a commander to
keep his men in a condition of inactivity, and he
selected Richfield as the initial point of a series
of assaults.

Selecting a dozen of his gang, including both
Frank and Jesse James, he placed them under the
leadership of Captain Scott, with orders to raid
the garrison.

Suddenly appearing, the desperadoes dashed into
the town, Frank James leading. A desperate conflict ensued, but the unerring marksmanship of the
guerillas, and their consummate qualities of dash,
won the day. Captain Sessions, and his lieutenant
Groffenstein, were killed the first volley. Ten of
the militiamen bit the dust, but the guerillas lost
not a man. The garrison immediately surrendered
to Captain Scott, who paroled the survivors.

The challenge thus thrown out by Quantrell was
accepted by the Union forces, who were immediately massed together for offense and defense.
Reinforcements were hurried forward, and elaborate
plans were made to crush the band of outlaws
under Quantrell.

In some manner, Mrs. Samuels became informed
of the plans that were being laid by the Feder-

als, and she waited impatiently for an opportunity
to forward the important news to Quantrell. This
chance was soon hers, for, one dark night, Jesse
James, who had been detailed as a scout by the
astute chieftain, after a long wearisome ride through
the wild county of Clay, came to his mother's
house.

She received him with open arms, her maternal
bosom swelling with pride as her desperado son
detailed the particulars of the Richfield raid.

The information she gave was of such important
nature, that before the first streak of dawn appeared,
Jesse was in the saddle again, speeding to Scott.

To him he told the news. The garrison of Plattsburg, in Clinton, was practically deserted, as the
soldiers were on a raid after the guerillas.

Scott speedily outlined a plan of operations,
and the sharp quick words of command "To saddle"
put the little troop in motion.

When within a few miles of Plattsburg, they
defiled into a dense bit of timber, and sent forward
scouts.

When these returned in the afternoon with their
reports, the freebooters again sprang into the saddle, and dashed toward the doomed town. Riding
straight for the market square, they found a few
militia-men in the court-house. At once all was
confusion, for, though taken by surprise, the soldiers were reluctant to surrender without resistance.

While the tumult was at its height, the Federal commander, Captain Rodgers, rode unsuspectingly into the square.

In an instant Frank James captured him, and the gallant soldier was a disarmed prisoner.

When his men saw their commander a captive, they poured volley after volley into the band of marauders. For a short time affairs assumed a serious aspect for the guerillas, and the issue seemed doubtful.

Frank James, who had turned his captive over to Captain Scott, appreciated the gravity of affairs and shouted to the Captain—"Captain, shoot that man . dead unless the garrison surrenders."

To this advice, Scott lent a willing ear, and drawing his ready revolver, swore to kill the officer unless he surrendered.

Captain Rodgers, although a brave man, saw that the guerillas held the winning hand, and hauled down his colors instanter, and his men and the town were in the hands of Scott's men.

Pillage and looting followed the victory. Several hundred muskets were part of the spoils, and besides a large quantity of clothing, $12,000 cash was secured.

Frank James secured $1,000, as his share of the plunder, and that day received from Scott, the first money from the proceeds of a raid his fingers had ever felt.

So elated was Scott with his bonanza victory,

that he determined to round out the day in a rather peculiar manner.

Paroling his prisoners, he ordered the principal hotel keeper of the place to prepare a banquet, and invited the Federal commander, his troop and some citizens to join the feast. The affair was a huge success, the foes of the afternoon ate, drank and sang together in the evening, and the "feast of reason and flow of soul" continued until nine o'clock. Then, with a parting song, a farewell yell, and a boisterous chorus, the dare-devils leaped into their saddles, and plunged into the darkness, making their swift way to Quantrell's camp.

Although a guerilla chief, commanding men of unbridled passions and brutal license, Quantrell was a strict disciplinarian. He ruled his force with a rod of iron, and exhibited such remarkable qualities of military order, that to his men, his name was but another synonym for success.

His standard was a black flag, made by the sweetheart of one of his freebooters, and the dark folds of the terrible insignia proved a veritable black curse wherever it was unfurled. Brooking no act of disobedience, exacting from his men the strictest fidelity and constant loyalty to himself, terribly swift in his punishments, Quantrell held his wild ungovernable border ruffians in the leash, and made them as plastic clay in the potter's hands. When he said "Do this," it was done;

"Go" and they went; "Come" and they came. No consideration of the value of life prevented them from obeying his slightest command.. No danger was too great, no privations too hard, for these Quantrell's guerillas. They belonged to him, and him alone, body and soul.

Banded together in the closest free-masonry, sworn to fealty by the most terrible oath the inventive ingenuity of their captain could devise, they stood or fell together, vieing with the followers of Mahomet in fanatical devotion to their leader and each other.

Quantrell was really a man of rare intellect and masterly mind. He combined the highest type of executive ability with the rashest of bravery, and now fairly enlisted in his self-chosen cause, he threw his whole soul into the work and flashed over the terror stricken land, a flame of destruction.

Jesse James thus become imbued with the same characteristics which distinguished his captain. His youthfulness was no bar to his expansion, on the contrary, his mind was in condition to receive and assimilate the ideas, characteristics and ethics which emenated from and controlled the rough existence he loved so well. The seed fell upon fruitful ground, and in the fiery heat of fierce passions it rapidly matured.

The crack of the revolver, the flash of the keen bowie knife and the intoxicating dash of his swift

steed become the sweetest and most fascinating
sensations.

His unquestionable bravery and reckless fidelity
to his comrades, soon won the affections, not only
of Quantrell, but of the fierce outlaws as well, and
he was often selected to lead forays and plundering expeditions.

The condition of affairs in Western Missouri at
this time were deplorable. The country was over-
run by soldiers. Both Federals and Confederates
swarmed, and, on all sides, hung the dark bands of
the lawless guerillas, gleaning after the destruc-
tive harvesters. No man's life was safe, and no
woman's honor but what was in jeopardy. Rape, murder, robbery and assassination strode through the
devoted land, and their hellish foot-prints were
used as graves for their victims.

Quantrell's band, however, did not, at this time,
commit any of the petty crimes perpetrated by the
smaller gangs of outlaws. It was better organized
and numerically stronger, having some 200 men in
it. Although an irregular organization, it made
some claim of being regular Confederate troops,
enlisted in the cause, and acting under orders as
a detached corps. It is safe to admit this as true,
but the orders came from Quantrell, and Quantrell
alone. This was the condition of affairs in Western
Missouri, in August, 1863.

CHAPTER IV

QUANTRELL'S CAMP

A DIABOLICAL CONFERENCE—"ON TO LAWRENCE"—
THREE HUNDRED DEMONS LOOSED—TWO DAYS OF
BLOOD—THE MASSACRE OF LAWRENCE—
JESSE AND FRANK JAMES KILL SIXTY-
FIVE PERSONS—A CARNIVAL
OF HELL

Quantrell now had his force under good discipline, well armed and well mounted. The recruits which flocked to his standard swelled the band to three hundred men ready for the word.

After his victorious raid on Plattsburg, the sagacious captain moved his camp further south, and, ever after, constantly changed his headquarters.

Success had smiled upon him, and he began to believe himself invincible. The small game he had been hunting lost its blandishments, and his ambitious eyes swept the country in search of larger game more worthy his steel.

The guerillas were in camp one August evening, sitting around the cheerful camp fires; sentries were posted, videttes on horseback were stationed at remote distances, with keen eyes and alert ears, ready on the instant to speed back and give warning of an approaching foe. Circled around the camp, dimly outlined in the fitful gleam of the fires, ranged the darling horses of the bold raiders, and their owners, stretched upon the green sward, under the hospitable roof of the arching tree limbs, threw the elusive dice, or wagered their wealth upon the fascinating poker hand.

At a little distance, somewhat apart from the rest, a group of men in consultation could be observed. They were Quantrell, Frank and Jesse James, the Younger and the Shepherd brothers, and two or three other kindred spirits.

A conference was in progress which was diabolical in its object. Yet the quiet tones, guarded and low, of the speakers, gave no clue to the dastardly subject of their conversation.

Quantrell had selected Lawrence, a small but vigorous town in Kansas, situated on the river Kaw, as the objective point for a raid,.

His men were weary of small affrays, and this would serve a double purpose. It would give vent to the pent-up activity of the men and, at the same time, allow Quantrell to repay an old score, for Lawrence was the home of Gen. Jim Lane, the organizer and leader of the notorious Jayhawkers.

Rapidly outlining his plan, Quantrell put the matter to vote, and the result was an enthusiastic, and unanimous affirmative.

The element of extreme danger which entered into the proposed expedition, made it the more

desirous, and the possibility of a glorious revenge
on their old and hated foe made the leaders eager
to start.

The question was then put to the men, and a
stentorian yell of approval greeted the ears of their
leader.

Accordingly, at day break of the 19th of August,
the command, "Mount!" was given, and the cavalcade, three hundred strong, started on their march
for Lawrence.

The following two days were days of blood.
Terrible, fearful agonizing blood. As the frontier
man, wending his way through the trackless forests,
scars the trees with his ax, so that he will find his
path on the return march, so these border ruffians
blazed a path through the beautiful Kansas country, marking every turn, halt and digression by a
wanton murder or a cruel assassination.

In the route they took was the little town of
Aubrey, nestling on the border line of Kansas.
From this hamlet, Quantrell took three men whom
he saw sitting before a store, and compelled them
to accompany his band as guides.

Rendering their captor faithful service, the
fidelity induced by fear, they brought the whole
force, safely and expeditiously to Cole Creek, eight
miles from Lawrence, and were amply rewarded by
the facetious guerilla. Their reward was death, for
Frank and Jesse James, obeying the stern com-

FRANK JAMES.

nand, led the doomed men to a little grove near
at hand, and shot them down like dogs.

The 21st of August smiled on the beautiful land-
scape. The glorious sun shone down on a scene of
quietness and repose.

The town of Lawrence, proud of its young
strength, awoke to labor and the day's work.

Blissful ignorance was theirs, ignorance of impending disaster. The children played in the quiet
streets, and the housekeepers were busy in their
domestic pursuits. The men had gone to the shop,
store, and farm, and everything reflected content-
ment and plenty.

But yonder, in those woods, eight little miles
from the happy town, a long line of mounted men,
serpented its way through the trees. Like a huge
and slimy anaconda, it twined and writhed, each
second bringing it nearer and nearer its prey.

Slowly it approached, cruel in its leisure, until
it entered the confines of the town, then suddenly
a black flag swept past, a piercing yell hurtled
through the startled air, there was the swift rush
and direful thunder of horses' hoofs, and Lawrence
stood before her destroyers.

The folds of the dreaded flag told the terrified
people who the horsemen were, and overpowered by
fear, they stood trembling, or rushed blindly,
wildly, in every direction. But bullets are swifter
than feet, and on all sides the demonical crack of
the revolver told of death. Men, women and

children were made living targets for these creatures of hell. The cry of the wounded was drowned by the coarse oaths of the murderer, and the prayers of the women and pleadings of the men were answered by ribald facetiousness, preliminary to the fatal bullet.

The guerillas were intoxicated with blood. Their excitement at fever-heat, they lost all semblance to man, and became incarnate devils.

In this dreadful pandemonium, Jesse James, and his brother Frank, were especially conspicuous. The youngest of the band, they bore themselves like veterans. On every hand their steady aim and ready pistol sought for victims. Sixty five human beings were sent before their maker by these two men. Jesse James shot thirty and Frank thirty-five.

Quantrell lost no time in killing other people. He left such trifling matters to his subordinates. His heart was set on one object, and that object was Gen. Jim Lane, the leader of the Jay-hawks.

Every house, barn, nook and corner was searched by the energetic guerillas, but Lane had hid himself, like the dastard and coward that he was, in a safe and secure cornfield.

Foiled in this, his chief aim, Quantrell became furious. He gave the order to fire the town, "Spare women and children" he cried, "but death to every man, and hell take their houses!"

Jesse James and his Band 3

Then was hell indeed let loose, when the men found that Jim Lane had escaped them. The torch was applied, and the little Kansas town was soon in ashes, while the fleeing inhabitants were shot down like rabbits.

All day long this canrival of hell lasted, all day long murder and rapine stalked through the town, and destruction claimed it for its own. At last night, blessed, merciful night came, and Quantrell withdrew his men, but Lawrence was no more. Where once stood the houses was now smoldering ashes, and the ghastly faces of the murdered ones stared with dead eyes, into the cold night, while the evening breeze bore the sound of wailing, deep bitter weeping, on its wings.

But Quantrell heard it not. He was fleeing, pursued but escaping to his Missouri fastness. Peril beset him on every side. The Kansas militia and Federal regulars joined forces in the chase, and though seven thousand men were at his heels, Quantrell crossed the line and was soon safe in Clay County.

But twenty men were lost from the band in this raid: Is it to be wondered that Quantrell should boast that his life was charmed, and that defeat would never be his?

CHAPTER V

QUANTRELL'S GUERILLAS REORGANIZED

MRS. SAMUELS AS A SPY—A FATAL AMBUSCADE—THE
MURDER OF CAPTAIN RANSOME—SEVENTY FED-
ERALS SLAUGHTERED—FORTY KILLED
IN KANSAS—A PITCHED BATTLE
THE GUERILLAS VIC-
TORIOUS

For over a month Quantrell kept within his retreat, but his busy mind was planning new cam-
paigns, envolving future combinations. He resolved
to re-organize his force, dividing it into small
squads of twenty or thirty men,   each squad under
a capable officer. By so doing he could cover an
immense area of country, moving with increased
celerity because of the comparatively small number
to be moved. Jesse James was appointed commander of one of these squads, and twenty five men
were detailed under him.

Shortly after his appointment, he was informed
by his mother, Mrs. Samuels, whose sharp eyes
and keen ears were ever on the alert to discover
the movements of the Federal troops, that a company of soldiers in the blue uniforms, under the
command of Captain Ransom,   were to set out for
Pleasant Hill. So accurately was the informa-

tion given, that Jesse knew the hour they were to start and the route over which they would march.

His plans were soon made and speedily put into execution. An ambuscade was made, and when Captain Ransom was well in the confines of a deep wood, Jesse gave the word, and from a score of hidden rifles, the unerring bullets of the bandits' were hurled into the ranks of the doomed Federals.

So sudden and unexpected was the attack, that the Union troops were thrown into confusion, which was increased when a second volley was poured upon them. Then came the wierd guerilla yell, the fierce charge, and impetuous, irresistable rush of horsemen. No mercy was shown by the victorious freebooters, and the remnants of the Union cavalry turned and fled. Out of one hundred men who were marching toward Pleasant Hill, less than thirty returned, while Jesse James lost but one man.

His brother Frank, who fought under him, boasted of eight men who had fallen from his fire, while Jesse vaunted of seven.

A week had scarcely passed, and both Frank and Jesse James, at the head of fifty men, scored another victory for the black flag.

The affray occurred in Bourbon county, Kansas, about five miles from Fort Scott. Captain Blum, a Federal officer, commanding a company of seventy-five mounted infantry, was traversing the country road, when suddenly a wild yell broke upon their

ears, and the guerillas were upon them. Again
and again the dreaded revolvers spoke, and forty
Union men sank from their horses, killed by outlaw
bullets. Utterly demoralized, the Federals fled,
leaving their dead upon the field, to be despoiled
by their inhuman murderers.

Up to this time Quantrell's men had things their
own way. Their peculiar tactics, sudden appear-
ances and unerring revolvers had won them succes-
sive victories in the easiest manner, but, the next
affray in which the James brothers were engaged
was more in the nature of a pitched battle.

George Ford was in command of the guerillas
this time, with the James brothers as lieutenants.

They attacked a strong company of the Second
Colorado Cavalry, under a Captain Wagner. Pursuing their usual tactics, the guerillas first fired
from ambush, and then charged, but Captain Wagner, rallying his men, reformed them, and met the
bandit charge by a counter-charge. The conflict
became a hand to hand affair. Sabers were used,
and the rebel yell was answered by Union cheers.
Again and again Ford hurled his men against the
little force in blue, and again and again the plucky
Federals resisted the onslaught. Jesse James fought
like a demon. Giving his horse free head, with a
revolver in one hand and a sword in the other, he
was always in the very thickest of the fight.
Cleaving his way frantically through the wall of
Colorado men, he reached the side of Captain Wag-

ner, and, taking advantage of a chance opportunity, he drew on that gallant officer, and sent a bullet through his heart.

With the loss of their captain, the troops became demoralized, and fled. With brutal ferocity, the guerillas deliberately killed all the Union wounded, either by the bullet or with the sword, leaving their bodies to rot on the open prairie.

CHAPTER VI

FRANK JAMES ON A SCOUT

HE KILLS TWO MEN—THE BATTLE OF HARRISONVILLE—
QUANTRELL REPULSED—DEFEATED AGAIN AT
FLAT ROCK FORD—JESSE WOUNDED—
SAVED BY HIS COMRADES—QUAN-
TRELL·SUFFERS A DISASTROUS
DEFEAT—A GALLANT
DEED

This fresh outrage spurred the Federals to renewed activity, and their forces were massed upon Harrisonville, ready for an offensive and energetic campaign against Quantrell.

The latter sent Frank James to ascertain their position, number and disposition. The perilous task was awarded Frank because of his bravery and craftiness. He rode directly for Harrisonville, until he was within sight of the Union pickets.

Awaiting until the night set in, he left his horse concealed in a belt of timber and started on his scout. Finding a negro who was well informed, he drew from him all the desired facts and then started back to his horse. Before reaching the animal he was discovered by two of the guards, who challenged him. He answered them with his revolver, killing one and mortally wounding the

39

other, then, leisurely mounting, he rode away leaving the camp in an uproar.

Two days after this escapade, August 16th, 1864, Quantrell made an attack upon the Harrisonville garrison, and met with defeat.

The soldiers, warned fore-hand, were ready, and repulsed the guerillas with great loss.

Suffering the throes of humiliation, the chagrined outlaws withdrew, venting their spleen in deep oaths, and anxious to redeem themselves.

Hearing that a band of Union volounteers were encamped near Flat Rock Ford, they pushed on in that direction and again inglorious defeat was their reward.   Here Jesse James received his first wound, and but for the fidelity of his comrades it would have been his last.

A musket ball struck him on the breast, passing through and tearing away a portion of his left lung.

He fell from his horse, apparently lifeless, but, at the risk of their own lives, sacred to their oath, Arch Clement and John Janette rode back in the face of the terrible volleys, and rescued the fallen man.   He was carried to the home of a sympathizer and for many days hovered between death and life, but his magnificent constitution pulled him through, and by the first week in September, he was able to mount his horse, and fight again

On the 16th day of this month, while on his way to Kearney he shot and killed three men who opposed his way, and the next day rode twenty-nine miles to give Todd tidings of the Federal forces.

Three days after, the 20th of September, Quantrell's band met with a disastrous defeat.

The whole force made an attack on Fayette, Missouri. Quantrell and Anderson commanded, with Poole, Clements and Todd in charge of divisions. Every charge of the guerillas was met and repulsed by the Federals, who stood their ground in the face of the most furious onslaughts. Time and again Quantrell hurled his troops against the Union forces, and time and again they withdrew, leaving dead and wounded before the victorious blue coats.

Jesse James redeemed the defeat in part by a noble action, in rescuing Lee McMurtry, one of Anderson's dare-devils, who fell, fearfully wounded, right under the guns of the Federals.

Despite the terrible risk, Jesse rode back in the face of almost certain death, and dragged his friend into safety. It was a gallant deed, worthy a better cause.

CHAPTER VII

AN UPRORIOUS DEBAUCH STILLED—TEN MEN DELIBER
ATELY SLAUGHTERED—A SICKENING SPECTACLE
—FRANK SAVES A LAD—A DEED OF
MERCY—A DAY OF BLOOD—A
MASSACRE AT CENTRALIA
—THIRTY-FIVE UNION
MEN KILLED

Four miles east of Wellington, in Lafayette
County, there stood a road house, filled with
courtesans and coarse women of ill-repute. Their
patrons, at this time, were the Federal soldiers
quartered near the locality, and the place became
notorious on account of the shamelessness of the
inmates, and the flagrant indecency of their
debaucheries.

One night, Quantrell detailed Frank James, and a
squad of five men to "raid the joint."

Arriving within a short distance, Frank halted his
men, and dismounting, stealthily crept forward to
reconnoitre. Through the chinks of the walls, he
peered into the house, and saw the place was full of
soldiers. Eleven of them were engaged in carrying
on a Bacchanalian carnival, ably assisted by the fair
damsels, who threw off their morals as they did
their clothing, for they were nearly all naked.

The scene presented to the eye peering into the room was one of vulgar voluptuousness in its most shameful degree. Locked in each others embrace, the nude revelers whirled around the low room, shouting and yelling in the very extreme of utter abandon. Lewd songs and ribald choruses were roared, and the fiery whiskey was quaffed like so much water. Faster and more furious grew the fun, and the bagnio became the scene of an uproarious debauch; when suddenly, shrill yells resounded without, and the Bacchanalians were instantly sobered. They knew the meaning of that unearthly yell.

"The guerillas! The guerillas!" shrieked the women, rushing aimlessly about the house.

The door was opened with a crash, and, revolver in hand, Frank James appeared to the terrorized debauchees.

"Come out here, you men," he shouted, "every d—d one of you. You sluts," he said to the women, "dry your yapping, you're too d—d dirty to touch."

Resistance was useless, and ten of the men passed outside. They had scarcely passed the door when a volley was poured into them, and every man dropped where he stood.

Frank James, who had counted eleven men and eleven women, at once instituted a search for the eleventh man, but he could not be found. Then Frank noticed there were twelve women, and, searching further, found the man. He was but little more than a boy, a lad with beardless face and blue eyes. He was the lover of one of the creatures there, who deftly and quickly threw a dress on him at the first alarm, and he would have passed or a woman but or Frank's sharp eyes.

In vain the women prayed and pleaded. The boy was dragged forward to the redoubtable leader. As he passed by, he could see the forms and faces of his ten comrades, still and stiff in the ghastly moonlight. Such would be his fate, and his heart failed him. As he came to Frank, the poor lad trembled in every limb.

"Come along," said Frank, "and be shot."

With a terror-stricken heart, the lad followed the cold blooded murderer to a thicket near at hand.

"Here's a good place," said James, looking coolly at his revolver.

"Oh, spare me, spare me!" pleaded the poor fellow, "I never did you any harm. Let me go for my mother's sake. It would break her heart if I should die this way, and near that house."

For a second Frank looked at him, the bright moon weaving its way through the leaves fell upon the tear-stained face of the lad. Cocking his revolver he slowly drew it up, and fired it over the boy's head.

"Go, boy!" he said, and returned to his command.

This deed of mercy Frank James kept to himself. It would be difficult to determine what change of heart, acting so suddenly, brought about the merciful deed, but, as he afterwards said:

"I reckon the old woman was glad to get her kid back safe."

The 27th of September, 1864, came. One of the darkest days in the history of Missouri, and a day ever to be remembered with tears, curses, and shudderings by the inhabitants of Centralia.

Bill Anderson, a human tiger in the guise of a man, was the bravest, most desperate, bloody and atrocious of all Quantrell's men. He was next in command, and even, at times, ranked equally with the guerilla chief. He resolved, for some fancied wrong, to perpetrate a massacre upon Centralia.

This little village was in the northwestern part of Boone county, on the line of the St. L. K. & N. R. R.

Before the Centralians had the first inkling of their approach, the guerillas, one hundred and fifty strong, dashed through their streets.

It was the repetition of other such scenes; wanton slaughter; reckless taking of life; rifled domiciles, and outraged women. Every house was pillaged, and the inhabitants driven out. Then Anderson drew his villainous crew up in line before the railway station. A train came along with five coaches well filled with passengers, soldiers and citizens. At once the passengers were ordered from the cars, and made to form a line.

Separating the soldiers from the civilians, they

were marched a little distance, when, at the sharp command, the ever fatal revolvers spoke, and thirty-five men in the blue uniform of the Union fell dead without a groan.

The remaining passengers were then robbed, and allowed to go on their way.

This scene had scarcely been enacted, before another drama took place. The guerillas were suddenly attacked by a body of Iowa volunteers under Major Johnson, who had ridden into town.

A fierce and bloody conflict ensued, and for a time, it looked as if the Iowans would win, but George Todd, intrepid and desperate, burst through the lines, followed by Jesse and Frank James, and soon the poor Federals were routed. Jesse, who had marked Major Johnson as his game, drew near him, and sent a bullet through his heart.

This ended the fray. The remaining Unionists fled in every direction leaving seventy of their number on the field.

One hundred and fifteen men were killed that day by Anderson and his bandits. Can anyone marvel that the devil takes care of his own?

But the day of retribution was coming, slowly, ah! so slowly, but it was coming. The tide of fortune turned against the guerillas shorty after the James brothers induced an old man by the name of Banes, to accompany them a short distance from his home; need it be said they ruthlessly butchered him?

They shot him down like a cur, and left his corpse, with its grey hair outlined against the dark road, for the next passer by to discover.

The tide was turning. Quantrell's band was gradually breaking up. Too many of the company had fallen to rise no more on earth. Death had been rather busy, and the task of digging graves was laborious. Jesse James was wounded again. George Todd was killed in a skirmish, and before December had closed, Quantrell had followed his trusty lieutenant to that home from which no man returneth. He died in captivity, fighting to the last, pierced by many bullets, at last falling with an empty revolver and a broken sword. Mortally wounded, he was captured by his foes, who, more humane than himself, conveyed him to a hospital, and he breathed his last, beside the falls of the Ohio, in Louisville.

CHAPTER VIII

A DASH INTO INDIAN TERRITORY

GREEK MEETS GREEK—A PITCHED BATTLE BETWEEN GU-
ERILLAS—JESSE KILLS CAPTAIN GOSS—A DES-
PERATE CHANCE—THE LEAP FOR LIFE—
MURDER OF HARKNESS—THE GUER-
ILLAS SURRENDER—JESSE AGAIN
WOUNDED

Strangely enough, neither of the James boys
were with their chief when he fought his last
battle. Jesse had gone with George Shepard and
fifty men, for a raid through Texas, and Frank
James had left, a few days previous to the affray,
for a visit.

It was late in the Fall of this terrible year of
1864, terrible in its results for poor bleeding
Missouri, that George Shepard, taking Jesse James
and half a hundred of the most desperate of Quantrell's band, left Missouri for Texas.

The trail through the Indian Territory was beset
by perils, and eternal vigilance was the order of
the day. The Indians were on the warpath against
such intruders as the freebooters, and, if the guerillas were desperate and brave the Indians were
crafty and cruel.

For a time the outlaws pursued the even tenor of

their ways unmolested. Their large number and perfect discipline, together with their well known courage caused them to be respected.

This comfortable condition of affairs lasted until the last of November, when they found their path blockaded by a band of Union troops—militia—under Capt. Emmett Goss. The band was a quasi-guerilla organization, celebrated through Texas for its wild daring, and audacious bravery. It was a case of "Greek meet Greek",

Goss was just returning from a wild raid through Arkansas, and had been emminently successful. The consequence of this chance meeting was a wild sanguinary contest. Both commanders, Shepard and Goss were tried veterans in irregular warfare, and their men were desperate and reckless. Like two ferocious dogs about to fight, the two companies faced each other, slowly circling around, each trying to get the slight advantage of position.

Then came a simultanous yell, and with a crash of thunder, the *melee* began. Back and forth the contestants rushed, turned and returned and charged.

Again and again the demoniac yell of Quantrell's men was answered by the wild shouts of the Texans. But Shephard won, for Jesse James, who fought like a tigress despoiled of her whelps, forced his furious way towards Capt. Goss, and, in quick succession, put two bullets into him. One through the brain and the other through the heart.

Jesse James and his Band 4

Elated with their victory, Shepherd's command resumed its march over the beautiful prairies of the Indian Territory. It was a perilous journey. The Cherokee Indians were favorable to the Union troops, and Shepherd's command was continually harrassed after his victory over Goss.

The hawk-eyed red-men surrounded him on all sides, and his men continually held their arms for in-stant service. At any time, a band of their redskin antagonists might appear around a belt of timber, and the fearful war-whoop resound in their ears. To stray from the column was hazardous in the ex-treme, as Jesse James discovered, nearly at the cost of his life.

Two days after the affray with the Texans, Jesse was riding alone, skirting the banks of a stream. His horse was tired, and he was looking for a good place to dismount and rest, when, without previous warning, a band of Cherokee Indians came in sight. As soon as he was discovered, they raised their war-whoops, and dashed after him in furious pursuit. They were speedily mounted, and Jesse knew they were sure shots. There was nothing for him to do but to run for it.

Clapping the cruel spurs into the sides of his exhausted horse, he fled, but soon found the pursu-ing Indians gaining. He was alone on the prairie. No friendly thicket, no cottonwood belt offered pro-tection. No band of comrades was at hand to aid.

He was alone on a horse already tired out.

There was but one chance, a desperate chance for him. He must leap a precipice which fell down to a stream. Sure death behind, a trifling chance before, and he took it.

Straight for the rocky ledge he rode, and, with a shout of defiance, both rider and horse leaped into awful space.

But Jesse James bore a charmed life, and his horse fell into a deep pool of water, and was not injured. He regained the land, and making a wide detour, reached camp in safety.

After spending a quiet winter in Texas, Shepherd broke camp, and set back for Missouri, experiencing a great deal of trouble from the Indians on the march. Hardly had the guerillas arrived in their beloved Missouri, when the devoted state knew that its old pests were returned. At once the machinery of murder and assassination was started, and April of '65 placed another cold-blooded deed against Jesse James' record.

James Harkness, of Benton County, had, all through the war, been a fearless, outspoken Unionist. He displayed his opinions openly and courageously, ever expressing them with reckless disregard for his life.

He was especially outspoken against the dastardly outrages committed by Quantrell's men, and was particularly bitter in his denunciations against the James brothers.

Jesse, aided by twelve of his comrades, captured

Harkness, and, while his two friends held him, Jesse coolly and deliberately drew his keen bowie knife across the Union man's throat, and threw the dead body into the ditch.

A few days after, another Union man of the same type was ruthlessly slaughtered by Jesse James, in spite of gray hairs and pleading prayers. This occurred near Kingsville, Johnson County.

In May, 1865, a number of guerillas surrendered to the United States authorities, with certain of the Confederate troops, but Jesse James refused and, with a small number of choice spirits, continued to range the country as of old. On one of these forays, they ran against a body of Federal troops, who immediately charged, and a furious fight commenced. The bandits suffered an irredeemable defeat. Jesse receiving another severe wound in the lung, and was left in the woods for dead. But again he recovered, and finally joined his brother in Nebraska, where he remained until he had recovered to some degree, when he journeyed back to Missouri, and was secreted in his mother's house.

CHAPTER IX

The narrator of this little sketch has no desire to pose as an apologist for Jesse James or his elder brother, Frank. He has no wish to lessen the approbrium attached to their names. He does not justify any of their deeds.

He recognizes the undeniable fact that they were bad, cruel, villainous murderers, whose hands were fairly reeking with innocent blood.

At the same time, justice and candor compels him to bear testimony to their courage and bravery. He cannot help but admire their superb horsemanship; and their unequaled skill with fire arms.

They seldom hesitated to meet the greatest odds against them, relying on these latter qualifications to carry them through unscathed, and the wonder inspired by the narration of their wild exploits is

53

increased, when it is remembered that both were young men. Frank James was but twenty-four, and Jesse a mere lad of twenty.

Yet they were already old veterans, tried and experienced campaigners. The voice of the revolver, the ping of the rifle ball, the ringing clash of swords, and the wild glare of battle were familiar to their ears and eyes.

For four years they had led roving, desperate and ensanguined lives. They had been hunted and followed through wild morasses, and over vast plains.

The cold biting winds of winter, and the fierce heat of the summer's sun had bronzed their skins, and hardened their bodies.

The tumult of battle and the mad excitement of the guerilla charge had kept their blood at a fever heat, and they were tired of it all. Innumerable wounds, and hard privations had had a salutory effect, and the young outlaws wanted rest.

But how cruelly true it is that "circumstances alter cases," and that a pebble, thrown by a baby hand, may change the current of a mighty river.

Jesse was home with his mother, recuperating after the damaging results of his last affair, while Frank, who had been paroled at Samuel's Depot, Kentucky, in July, was still in that state.

Like Jesse, he had grown weary of the passions and strife of war, and, with a firm determination to settle down, gave his parole to the proper authorities, and so, was included in the Amnesty Act.

The termination of the war let loose upon the community, the great mass of camp followers, guerillas, bush whackers, and camp-bummers who had hung on the skirts of the contending armies, as the skulking jackals follow the lion, picking up and fighting over his leavings, preying on all sides, irrespective of partisanship.

The cessation of hostilities took the regular troops from the field, and the irregulars found their occupation, or rather opportunites gone.

This being the case, they turned their undivided attention to robbing and pillaging anything from a hen-coop to a bank. Horse-stealing especially flourished and the farms and stock raisers of Kentucky suffered from their depredations.

Brandenburg, a town in Mead County, on the Ohio River, was a sort of rendezvous for the gentry who were so careless with other people's horses, and the surrounding country was up in arms, and indignation rose to a white heat.

As Frank James, mounted on his splendid charger, entered the town, he was noted. He was a stranger, and was bestride as fine a bit of horse-flesh as ever pleased the tastes of the Kentuckians, and this, to their suspicious eyes, was *prima facie* evidence that he was a horse-thief.

He entered the town quietly, ignorant of the prevailing sentiment, and proceeded to make himself comfortable at the hotel.

He was sitting quietly in the office of the caravansary, when his peaceful revery was rudely broken by the abrupt entrance of five men, well armed, and determined.

The leader,—a fine specimen of manly form, stepped up to the unsuspicious ex-guerilla, and placing his hand on his shoulder, remarked: "I arrest you as a horse-thief!"

At once Frank grasped the situation, but, accustomed to such sudden dangers, he betrayed no fear or excitement. There was nothing about him to alarm his would-be captors. He was a young man of twenty five, bronzed by the sun, and attired in ordinary clothing, so, without undue harshness, the leader of the posse, said, almost pleasantly:

"Will you consider yourself under arrest?"

"I consider no such proposition." was the rather unexpected reply, and before a movement further could be made, his quick hands sought and found his revolvers, there was a double report, closely followed by a third, and three men were writhing in mortal agony upon the floor. The remainder of the posse fled; but one, as he ran, ventured a shot, which well nigh rid the world of Frank James. The shot made a gaping wound in the hip, and Frank reeled in agony. But his blood was up. The old-time spirit was aroused, and he was again the relentless dare-devil of

Quantrell's band. Crawling to a post, he raised himself to an erect posture, and with his terrible eye, and more terrible revolver, held the aroused villagers at bay.

In the crowd which surrounded him, was a young man, one of the guerilla bands of the war, who recognized the wounded desperado holding the mob in check. With his horse the young fellow dashed forward and swinging Frank behind him, urged the steed to its utmost speed, followed by the imprecations and bullets of the angry and cheated populace.

His preserver took him to a safe hiding place, and nursed him back to health, but Frank never recovered from that chance shot, nor will he as long as he lives.

It was months of severe suffering for the wounded man, but he lived.

In the meantime the pebble which changed the course of Jesse James' destiny, was cast into his life stream.

He had but just sought the shelter of his maternal home, when the country was electrified by the news that the Commercial Bank of Liberty had been robbed of $70,000.

People immediately connected the James boys with the crime, but it is due to them to state that neither had any hand in it.

Frank lay dangerously wounded in Kentucky, and

Jesse, just out of bed from a severe wound, was too weak and feeble to think of such an attempt.

Be it as it may, the people said the James brothers had a finger in the pie, and that settled it, and a party of men, who had somehow learned that Jesse James was at his mother's house, determined to pay off some old scores, and deliver him up to the authorities.

So, on the night of the 18th of February, four days after the robbery, six well armed men rode up to the residence of Dr. Samuels.

Jesse, who was tossing on a fevered bed, upstairs, heard the sounds of hoofs, and his suspicions were aroused. They were confirmed when he heard the horsemen enter the yard, and knock loudly and emphatically upon the door.

Dr. Samuels answered the knock, pretending to have trouble with the lock, to gain time.

By this time Jesse was up and armed, and standing beside his step-father.

"What shall I do? whispered the old gentleman.

"Open the door when I tell you," and Jesse cocked both revolvers.

The knocking was renewed impatiently, and a rough voice shouted:

"Open this d—d door, or we'll smash in the panel."

"Have a second's patience," replied the doctor, "there's something the matter with the blamed lock, "bring out that murdering thief, Jesse James," yelled the knocker, "bring out the d—d scoundrel."

The answer came, and was disastrous, for, opening the door, Jesse fired with unerring precision, and two men fell, their blood trickling upon the white snow.

Then the other four saw the terrible figure full in the moonlight. His blazing eyes set in the white face, and glancing over the barrels of the trusty revolvers. Again they spoke, and two more of the panic-stricken volunteers were sent to their last accounts.

The remainder, leaping on their horses, fled as if the imps of hell were at their heels, and riding back to town told their tale, detailing the awful facts with gross exaggerations.

A solemn determination was taken. The people had grown weary of this reckless blood letting, and it was determined that Jesse James must die.

Accordingly, fifty men, armed to the teeth, returned to Samuel's house, and demanded of Mrs. Samuels that Jesse be delivered up to them; but Jesse was miles away. Sick, and feeble as he was— trembling with fever, he had mounted his horse, had gone to a safer and more retired locality. Waiting a few days to recover as much strength as possible, he started on a long and painful journey for Kentucky, where he found Frank, still suffering from his wounded hip. But still Jesse did not recover. For months he lay upon a sick bed, suffer-

ing untold agonies.   At last, he determined to seek
the best medical attention, and in October of 1867,
went to Nashville and put himself under the care of
Dr. Paul F. Eve, a well known surgeon.

It was not until the spring of '68 that he felt
so far recovered that he could be considered con-
valescent.   He then joined Frank at Chaplin,
where the wounded outlaw was in hiding.

In this—their retreat, the two brothers took
council together.

The affair at Brandenburg, and Jesse's affray at
home, decided the course of their future lives.

Every crime of any magnitude, no matter in what
locality the crime was located, was charged to the
James brothers.   If a bank was robbed in Kansas,
and two hours later another was despoiled in
Kentucky, the James brothers did it.   If a man
was found dead, murdered, upon a lonely road in
Missouri, and a horse was stolen in Illinois, three
hundred miles away, it was the James brothers
that did it.

They had the name, and might as well have the
profits.   Every door was closed against them.
They knew it would be impossible for them to
return to Kearney openly, and live there.   The die
was cast ,and they determined to earn the reputation which had been given them.

The call was passed, and Jesse James and his
band of notorious outlaws were let loose upon the
country.

CHAPTER X

JESSE AND HIS BAND

COLE YOUNGER—JIM WHITE—GEORGE SHEPHERD—OLE
SHEPHERD—A SECRET SESSION—RUSSELLVILLE'S
BANK RAIDED, MARCH 1868—$100,000—
TAKEN—A MASTERLY RETREAT—
GEORGE SHEPHERD ARRESTED—
OLE SHEPHERD SURROUNDED
AND KILLED

It has never been accurately learned who composed
the first Jesse James band of raiders. The material
from which the young outlaw could select was plentiful; for, scattered all over Kentucky, Tennessee
and Missouri were members of the guerilla organi-
zations which played such an important part in
the war of the rebellion. Their well-known qualities
were highly appreciated by these irregular soldiers,
and if Jesse or Frank James passed the word along
the line for men, the responses would be prompt and
numerous.

It is safe to say, however, that Jesse selected
his timber with great care and after considerable
hard thinking. And, as members of Quantrell's band,
his own tried comrades-at-arms would naturally have
the preference, the assumption that Cole Younger,
Jim White, George and Ole Shepherd were with

him in his first exploit as a bank robber, would
not be far out of the way.

It was early in the year of '68, when the gang
finally gathered together at Chaplin, and into a
secret session as committee on ways and means, to
consult together on plans for the future. The
plans were not only elaborated, but speedily put into
execution.

Russellville was a thriving town of some four
thousand inhabitants in the southern part of Kentucky, nearly adjoining Tennessee, and was the
principle town in a large well-to-do district.

Its bank conducted a large business, and was
large in proportion to the size of the town. The
former season had been particularly good, the roads
were in an excellent condition, business was rushing, and in consequence, a large amount of money
was locked within its vaults.

On this bank the longing eyes of Jesse James were
turned, and his itching palms were eager to grasp
the wealth it held.

The morning of March 20th, '68 opened clear and
beautiful, and the little town had opened its stores
and was getting ready for the business of the day.

The bank was about to open its doors also, when,
down the long straggling main street a dozen horsemen appeared. Each rider was armed with two
pairs of revolvers, and as they rushed by, they
uttered deep oaths and outrageous imprecations,
threatening death to any man who should attempt

TWO AGAINST FORTY.

to hinder them in any way, ordering those on the street to go into their houses, under penalty of instant death.

Without halt or slacking of reins, the brigands rode straight to the bank, and two men, Jesse James and Cole Younger, leaped to the ground, and disappeared through the bank door.

The cashier had just opened the safe, and was arranging his papers, preparatory to the day's business, when he was suddenly confronted by two armed men, strangers to him.

Instantly the situation was appreciated, and he turned quickly to shut the safe, but a stern command accompanied by an eloquent gesture from Jesse James' revolver, halted him.

"Leave that alone and be quiet, or I'll blow your brains out!" was the peremptory command.

The cashier was a wise man. His life was more valuable to him and the community than the gold in the safe, and the shining barrels of the threatening revolvers rendered him powerless to do aught but comply with their gentle urgings.

In a jiffy both desperadoes were over the counter and the safe was rifled. Cole Younger swept up the loose change on the counter, and everything but some postage stamps were soon in the possession of the robbers.

The stamps were left, Jesse James facetiously remarking, "that he would leave them as the cashier might want to mail some letters later in the day."

With the booty in their possession, the two outlaws left the bank (which was about all they left),
and mounting their horses, swept back again over
the road, shouting dire threats to any one who
would dare follow. $100,000, was securred in this
simple manner. It was done in ten short minutes,
and the stunned citizens of Russellville could
hardly comprehend the fact that ten men had
boldly entered their tight, tidy town, robbed their
bank in open day, and departed without meeting
the slightest opposition.

The impudence and audacity of the raid was
almost inconceivable, and the celerity with which
the gang operated, suggested an intimate acquaintance with the locality and habits of the place, only
acquired by good preliminary work. It was a well
planned, ably-executed transaction; the bloodless
feature of the affair was due to the paralysis which
struck every able-bodied man in the town, when
they saw the ten dare-devils sweep so suddenly
down the street.

This paralysis was temporary however, for, hardly
had the robbers gained the outskirts of the town,
when the hue and cry was raised. At once a posse
was organized for the pursuit. The Kentucky blood
was at fever heat, and it was a well-armed, well-
mounted party of resolute, determined men who
struck the hot trail, and set off in keen and eager
pursuit of the saucy bandits.

Jesse James and his Band 5

But the latter were also well-armed and well-mounted. They, too, were resolute, determined men, and had for their leader, a young fellow, with a lion heart, an eagle's eye, an Indian's sagacious patience and the powerful aid of the devil himself.

For days the pursuing party followed the fleet desperadoes. Over the mountains, through the valleys, plunging into deep waters, tramping over unbroken fields, threading the dark forests and skirting broad rivers, until the Father of Waters, the wide, deep rolling Mississippi was reached, and stretched between the pursuers and pursued, for the robbers had crossed and plunged into the pastures of their own Missouri.

Still the Kentuckians kept the trail, but it became blinder and blinder, less and less distinct, until it was lost to view. Then, and only then, they gave it up, and returned, sadder and wiser men, to their native town.

Shortly after, however, George Shepherd was caught, and sent to the penitentiary for a long term of years. Susequently, Ole Sheperd was located in Jackson County, Missouri. The necessary papers were made out, and a posse of thirty men sent after him. They discovered his hiding place, and surrounding it, called on him to surrender, under pain of instant death.

"Surrender be d—d." was the old guerilla's reply. "Do your worst." and he fired the first shot.

The firing became general. There could be but one result, and the desperate bandit, fighting until every chamber of his revolvers was emptied, fell with seven bullets in his body.

He died defiant to the last, cursing his slayers with his last breath. The rest escaped for the time.

They lost little time in mourning for their imprisoned comrade, nor did they shed many tears for their fallen brother. It was a chance they took, and if the law claimed one victim, and relentless death another, what was it to them. They had secured over $10,000 each, as their share of the booty, and it paid to take such risks, as the compensation, if successful, was so great.

But the escape of the robbers, their long, wearisome retreat, the forced marches under the darkness of night, the thousand-and-one perils which sprang up to drag them down to the grave, the stealthy ride through sleeping villages, the sudden dashes across moonlit roads; sallies, skirmishes, hunger, thirst, and numberless hardships which beset them, speak volumes for their endurance and bravery.

No romantic robber-hero of olden times could compare with these modern bandits, and no romancer could depict, with the sorcery of his imagination, such a tale of almost incredible wonder. Yet, it is true, and it is here written, a plain unvarnished tale almost beyond belief.

CHAPTER XI.

After the Russellville bank robbery, Jesse James stole back to Kearney and was secreted in the Samuels homestead. The privations of the fearful ride from Russellville to Missouri told upon him.

There seemed to be no limit to his endurance, but this last affair reacted upon his health, and he was again an invalid.

Acting under the advice of some friends, he went to Kansas City, and consulted Dr. Joseph Wood of that place, an eminent and skillful practitioner.

The surgeon at once recommended a change of scene and air, and suggested a sea voyage, telling him to seek a warmer and more genial clime, where the shattered lung and debilitated system could recuperate.

Accordingly, Jesse James bade farewell to his family, and journeyed to New York. After spending a few days with friends, he set sail, June 9th, 1869 for Panama, and thence to San Francisco.

During this time, Frank James, still suffering from his wounded hip, which had not been helped to any great extent by his Russellville experience, was hiding in the house of a friend in Nelson County, Kentucky. Waiting until the excitement had blown over, he went to Louisville, and from there to Kansas City, where his mother was visiting. He then traveled overland to San Francisco, reaching that city in advance of Jesse.

The two brothers met at the home of their uncle, a Mr. D. W. James, who was proprietor of a hotel at Paso Robel.

For several months the young men lived there quietly and peacefully, conducting themselves with such circumspection, that no one dreamed the two quiet, gentlemanly young fellows were the twin devils of murder and pillage who had caused four states to tremble and quiver with horror at their very name.

It is said that so successful were the young bandits in thus disguising themselves, and so rapidly did they acquire the manners and polite modes of the fashionable watering place, that more than one susceptible maiden fell victims to their fascinations, and they became the leading beaux of the place.

How true this may be, can only be conjectured, but there they remained all summer, gathering health and strength, until they were completly restored. By the time this was fully accomplished, they had become restless, and it required but a slight incentive to start them on their travels. This came in the shape of several of their old comrades, whom they met.

With these they set out for the mining camps, and the slumbering fire of their old guerilla spirit was soon fanned into a flame, which needed but slight encouragement to develop into a fierce fire with a consuming heat.

There were many mining towns near Paso Robel, and further up the mountains, in the neighborhood of the new diggings, such towns sprang up, almost in a day—mushroom villages of uncertain life.

The discovery of a new find, or a rich formation caused the migratory miners—birds of impulse and passage, to flock to the locality.

Every nugget picked from some pocket was to be the key to some new El Dorado. The news would spread, and from all sides the eager diggers would rush to the golden portal, anxious to obtain fabulous wealth.

First the hasty shacks of the prospectors would spring up on some level plateau, or cling to the steep sides of a rugged bluff, then would follow the tents and canvas houses, then the inevitable saloon and dance hall would blossom forth in all their cheap tawdery, a store would follow, another saloon, a black-smith shop, then two more saloons, more dance halls, and then the incongruous jumble of tents, shanties, hastily thrown together frame houses, saloons, dance halls, and shops would be dignified with a name, and the new town, built in three days, was a reality. The class of people who flocked to such effervescent hamlets partook of the nature of the place.

They were of all kinds and conditions. The honest and dishonest, steady and unsteady, noble and debased; a boiling, changing mass of excited humanity, careless of themselves, their money, their morals and their lives.

The gamblers and the liquor dealers assumed aristocratic airs to themselves and were usually the chief men of the town. They thrived and flourished whether "pay dirt" was struck or not. They toiled not, and neither did they spin, and yet "I say unto you, that Solomon in all his glory" did not acquire his wealth with less effort than did the sporting gentlemen of the mining camp, or the dexterous dispenser of the intoxicating enchanter that passed under the multifarious name of "drinks".

It was to just such a town that Jesse and Frank James, with two Missouri gentlemen of their ilk, and congenial tastes honored with a visit. The young metropolis bore the euphonious name of Battle Mountain, and was accounted one of the "swiftest" towns on the range. They went purely and simply to see the place. They saw the place with the most innocent intentions in the world, mere curiosity.

For a few days they roamed around, and took in the diggings; a party of gamblers noticed the quart- tette, and not having that acquaintance with them which might have deterred them from their purpose, laid a plan to skin them of some of their wealth. The James boys were proud of their abilities as poker players. The fascinations of the draw were sufficient for them to accept the tender of a friendly game which the accomodating and friendly gam- blers made them, and, one evening found them seated around the table, with the pile of chips and elusive pasteboards before them.

For some time the game progressed without ex- citement, the Missouri men sitting together, and their quandom friends occupying the other sides of the table, while in the room were thirty others who were in the deep-laid scheme which was to despoil the ex-guerillas of their pile.

A jack-pot was on, cards had been drawn, one by one the players laid down their cards, until the game was reduced to two, a gambler of the town and one of Jesse James' party.

The gambler was in the plot, so when the Missourian called him, he cheerfully remarked, with a satisfied glance at the swollen and luscious pot.

"Three Kings."

"Three Aces," was the cool response, as the man from the States showed down his three single spots and calmly raked in the pot.

"I discarded a king," he continued, "when the cut was made for your deal, the bottom card was exposed. It was a king, so you got your three kings from the bottom. You mustn't do that again."

"You lie!" was the angry retort, and the gambler's hand sought his revolver, as his eyes flashed the mischief he was contemplating.

There was an ominous movement throughout the room. A sudden calm fell upon the place. A man had been accused of cheating, and the lie had been passed, and death was the penalty, according to the gambler's code of honor.

Jesse James, with his usual promptitude, grasped the idea instantly. He saw the nervous haste with which the gambler felt for his shooting iron, but, the hand of Jesse James was quicker, his aim was surer and when his ready revolver belched forth its death dealing flame, the gambler fell back, dead.

Quick as a flash, the other gambler sprang forward with a knife, and made a quick slash at Jesse, but quicker than a flash, the revolver swung round, and, with his brains spattering the wall, and the entire top of his head blown off, the card-playing sharp stretched his length upon the floor, a quivering corpse.

Then the slumbering hell awoke, and pandemon-

ium began; with a shout and a yell, the entire
crowd charged the four friends.   Forty men against
four.

Ranged shoulder against shoulder, fearless as a
tiger, cool as an iceberg, and calm as a mill-pond
the quartette faced their raging opponents.

Suddenly the lights were put out, and Jesse, between the cruel workings of his pistols, shouted:

"Stand aside!   Be ready."

Frank and the other two understood; with a rush,
they made for the door, Jesse covering the retreat
with his revolvers.   As soon as they had escaped,
they began firing into the howling, maddened
crowd, allowing Jesse to reach the door.   Two
brawny gamblers sprang upon him.   One sank with
a bullet in his brain, and the other, struck sense
less with the stock of the empty pistol, fell across
his comrade's body.   Leaping over this ghastly barricade, Jesse joined his friends outside, safe and
unscratched.

It was a murderous affair, and the men who thus
awoke the sleeping tiger were horror-struck when
they contemplated the awful scene after the
lights had been re-lit.   On the rough floor lay the
bodies of three dead men, and writhing in mortal
agony, five others were scattered about.   The floors
and walls were spattered with blood, and a huge
blotch near the door was the remains of the dead
gambler's brains.

Obeying a sudden impulse, one of those unexplainable sensations which seems to animate and move a great crowd, making each individual do the same thing at the same time, like a company of soldiers drilling, the wild mob of gamblers, hangers on, and miners rushed after the daring Missourians.

Scarcely had they run a mile, when they came within sight of the four men, leisurely moving out of the town. The self-appointed leaders of the pursuing crowd rushed forward, yelling, and crying for the James boys and their companions to stop.

"Fall back!" cried Jesse. "Fall back, we fought once for self-defence, and we will do it again."

But the yelling, cursing pack continued their headlong course. Again Jesse warned them.

"Back, you d—d fools! Stand back!"

This did not deter them, and they still made for the objects of their vengeance.

Then Jesse turned to his comrades.

"We are in for it again, boys, give it to them." Turning to the oncoming mob, he cried:

"Come on, d—d you. Come on, and get shot!"

Suiting his actions to the words, he pulled the trigger and a man plunged forward, headforemost to the earth. Three other shots rang out, almost simmultaneously with Jesse's, and three dead men dropped. Again the Missourians fired, and two more of their pursuers fell. Then the mob halted, wavered and turned. Jesse James and his companions were safe, and resumed their journey, but, they left behind fourteen dead and dying men as souvenirs of their visit. They had shaken up Battle Mountain as the town had never before, or after experienced.

CHAPTER XII

BACK IN MISSOURI

THE GALLATIN BANK RAIDED—THE CASHIER, JOHN W.
SHEETS, MURDERED—COLUMBIA (KY.) BANK OF
DEPOSIT ROBBED—A BRAVE CASHIER BRU-
TALLY BUTCHERED—BILL LONGLY SHOT
—CORYDON (IA.) BANK MULCTED
OF $40,000

The James brothers concluded that the Sierras
gold country was not a very salubrious and healthy
climate for them, after their little escapade at
Battle Mountain. The notoriety they acquired on
account of this trifling eccentricity was not compa-
tible with their best interests; and the publicity,
which is the penalty imposed on all noted men,
was inflicted on them, and grated on their modest
and retiring dispositions. For these reasons they
concluded that the finger of wisdom pointed to
their Missouri home, and after remaining in seclu-
sion a few days to allow the Battle Mountain
hurricane time to calm down, they started overland,
and, in due time, arrived in Missouri.

Reaching their old stamping grounds, they at
once—like the honest, hard working men they were—
looked around for employment. Money was no
object, it was employment they were after. It did

77

not take them a great length of time to find it,
and, letting their inclinations lead as they
wished, they determined to embark in the banking
business. Their last financial venture in that line,
at Russellville, had been eminently successful, and
with buoyant hopes, and sanguine dreams of again
filling their coffers, they surveyed the country for
a likely opening.

Organizing their company without any ostenta-
tious display or blowing of trumpets, they proceeded to put the machinery in operation. The place
was Gallatin, a thriving little burgh of Daviess Co.
Missouri. It was Russellville all over again, but
with the difference, that Russellville was a "clean
job"; the Gallatin affair was a "dirty" one, for innocent blood was shed with the recklessness of brutish
and depraved men.

On the 15th of December, 1869, a band of armed
horsemen entered the town of Gallatin, and urging
their animals down the main street with the veloc-
ity of the wind, flourished their revolvers, and
uttering curses and oaths, ordered the people to
stay in their houses. When the bank was reached,
two of the raiders sprang from their horses and
rushed into the bank. They were Jesse James and
Cole Younger.

The vault door was wide open, and one of the
men, pressing his revolver against the head of
the cashier, Capt. John W. Sheets, ordered him to
remain quiet. The other hastily secured the money

—a mere paltry amount—$700 or so—and placed it in a bag.

Captain Sheets, powerless and helpless, had remained a passive spectator of the outrage, but this did not save him, for, just as they were leaving, one of the outlaws (whether Jesse James or Cole Younger is not definitely known) deliberately leveled his revolver, and shot the cashier dead.

The ruffians left as they came, and vanished from sight leaving a rifled bank, and the rigid body of the murdered cashier prone upon the bank floor.

The unprovoked, cowardly assassination of Captain Sheets aroused the entire country, and the full force of the law was put into operation. The region round about was scoured and searched, pursuing parties found the trail, and chased the robbers to the borders of Clay County. There the marauders disappeared. They were on their native heath, and were safe.

The friends of the James brothers did all in their power to discredit the statement that they were implicated in this horrible affair. Jesse James had the supreme affrontery to write a personal letter to Gov. McClury denying that either he or Frank had any connection whatever with the Gallatin bank robbery and murder. But, as time brought forth new developments, the facts were well substantiated, that it was either Jesse James or Cole Younger who shot Captain Sheets.

Whether they were engaged in this robbery or

not, it is absolutely certain that they were active participants—the planners and leaders of the next one.

This time the scene of operations was transferred again to Kentucky, the scene of their first attempt at bank raiding.

Columbia, is the county seat of Adair County, Kentucky, and its bank was known to be a particularly thriving institution, doing considerable business, and handling a large quantity of money. It was about two o'clock in the afternoon of April 29th, 1872, that the President of the Bank of Deposit (for such was the name of the institution) was conversing with the cashier, Mr. R. A. C. Martin, and a citizen, Mr. Garnett, by name. An unusual commotion attracted their attention, and glancing out upon the street, they saw five horsemen riding furiously down the street. Before they could realize that anything out of the common was occuring, the door flew back, and the gentlemen were gazing into the barrels of four revolvers, held by the steady hands of Frank James and Cole Younger. Without a word, the two intruders passed around the counter, and presenting a pistol to the head of the cashier, one of them cried in a peremptory tone:

"Will you give up the safe keys, d—n you?

"I will not!" replied the plucky cashier.

"Then, G—d d—n you, will you open the safe?

Come, quick. I've no time to waste. Come now, I'll blow your d—d brains out. Will you?"

"I will not. I will d—"

The defiant words were never finished, for a bullet crushed his temple and his blood and brain spurted over the desk and the horrified President.

The two robbers saw the game was up. The cashier had the combination, and time was more precious than all the money in the bank. A murder had been committed, and they must flee. Hastily sweeping up the loose money on the counter, $300.00, they darted to the street, mounted, and the cavalcade of robbers and murderers swept from sight.

Pursuit was instituted at once, and excepting that one raider, Bill Longly, a new recruit from Texas, was shot in Fentress County, the gang again escaped.

Before twelve months had passed, the Jesse James gang again raided a bank. It was the bank in Corydon, Iowa. The day was the 28th, of June, 1873. It was the regular procedure. Twelve armed and mounted men suddenly dashed into town, terrorized the inhabitants, and held them away from the bank.

Three of the robbers entered the bank and, bringing six revolvers to bear on the officials, compelled them to pass out all the money. Then the rapid remount, the quick order, the hurry of flying hoofs, and then—.

6

$40,000, was the product of this last robbery, and not a cent was ever recovered, and not a man caught in the search instantly set in motion.

Russellville! Gallatin! Columbia! Corydon! $141,000! Two murders.   What a record.

CHAPTER XIII

KANSAS CITY FAIR

$10,000 SCOOPED BY JESSE JAMES—A BOLD, RECKLESS
AFFAIR—A CLEAN JOB—A BANK AT STE. GENE-
VIEVE ROBBED—A BOLD LEAP. A SLIGHT
MISHAP—A COWARDLY DOZEN

The two events to be recorded in this chapter, are placed here because it is popularly supposed that Jesse James and his dashing free-booters were the audacious gentlemen who participated in the affair; although, it is a mere matter of conjecture.

But the ear marks pointed to Jesse James; the characteristics of Russellville, Gallatin and Cory-don, were present in both the Kansas City and Genevieve raids, and it is a fair presumption to make that Jesse and Frank James were the leaders.

The robbery of the Kansas City Fair, was the most audacious, bold and reckless affair that ever startled the world. Sheer impudence, and une-qualed boldness carried the day, and seven men, surrounded by the throngs of people visiting the fair, in the wide-open day, swooped down, picked up $10,000, and dashed away, unharmed and without hindrance.

There was a big crowd at the Fair-grounds that day, September 20th, 1872. Ethan Allen, the

famous race horse, was to trot, and the event drew
a large number of the race track devotees to the
fair grounds.

Great masses of people were crowding through
the gates and filling the grand stand and enclosure.

The fair was doing a howling business, nearly
$10,000, being taken in as gate receipts.

Although it was after banking hours, Mr. Hall,
treasurer of the Association, had made arrangements to deposit the sum, and, placing the money
in a tin box, gave it to a trusted employe to
carry to the bank. The idea that any sane person
male or female, would attempt to steal this box
in broad daylight in the midst of so many thousand people, was preposterous, and Mr. Hall never
dreamed of such a contingency.

The young man left the office with his valuable
bundle, and proceeded down the street.

As he did so, seven men, well armed, trotted
leisurely down the street. They attracted attention
to be sure, but it was mere curiosity. The magnificent horses they rode were admired, and the majority of the spectators thought the cavalcade part
of the show.

So it was, but it was not down on the pro-
gramme.

Suddenly, at a command, the seven men put
spurs to their horses, and dashed recklessly
through the crowd, which opened right and left in
hurried attempts to escape being trampled to death.

JESSE'S LEAP FOR LIFE.

When the men were opposite the messenger carrying the tin box, they halted, and, drawing their revolvers swore to instantly kill any one making the slightest attempt to hinder them.

One tall, athletic man (supposed to be Jesse James) sprang from his horse, and thrusting his revolver in the face of the astonished and paralyzed messenger, snatched the box from his nerveless hands, vaulted lightly into the saddle, wheeled his horse and with a shrill whistle, dashed down the street at full speed, followed by the remainder of the raiders.

Ten thousand dollars in clean hard cash. Not a shot was fired, not a person was injured. It was a "clean job".

Of course they were pursued, but all the pursuers found was the empty tin box, hanging to a tree five miles away. The raiders had escaped.

For some time the gang lived on the proceeds of the Kansas City raid, but money "easy come easy goes", and their flattened purses was an incentive to urge them on to renewed efforts in their peculiar line, and Ste. Geneveive, the old Catholic town of Missouri, was selected as the victim.

It was in the spring of '73, and the cashier of the savings bank, together with a young man, his assistant, named F. A. Rogers, had just entered the bank, ready to open up for the day, when they were suddenly confronted by four armed men, who spoke to them thus:

"We have come to help you open the bank. Open the safe instantly, d—m you, we have no time to lose."

"I am helpless and can not resist you," replied Mr. Harris, the cashier, and he turned to the safe.

Meanwhile the young clerk, Rogers, who had shown signs of creating an alarm, was sternly commanded to keep still.

"I? What for?" he inquired.

"Not another word, you young devil. Keep still, if you don't want your brain blown out of your d—d head."

But young Rogers was plucky, and taking advantage of the moment, made a bold leap and sprang down stairs to the street.

As he fled, the man watching him fired, the bullet tearing the shoulder of his coat and grazing his chin.

By this time the safe was opened, and the booty secured. To the intense disappointment of the James gang, they found but $8.500, where they had fondly dreamed of $80.000 or even $100.000 After relieving Mr. Harris of his watch, they left the bank, mounted their horses, and fled.

A slight mishap, which well nigh proved disasterous, happened to them just as they were leaving the city.

One of their horses ran away, and the bag containing their booty, broke, spilling the gold in the streets

A German farmer passing with his team was compelled to chase and capture the horse, while the robbers, with their drawn pistols stood guard over the gold.

A dozen men had hastily secured arms, and now appeared in pursuit, but the bold, determined front presented by the bank raiders cooled their ardor, and they returned, leaving Jesse James and his companions to escape with their ill-gotten wealth.

CHAPTER XIV

A CHANGE OF OPERATIONS

BANKING TO RAILROADING—THE COUNCIL OF WAR—
WATCHING THROUGH THE NIGHT—WRECKING THE
ROCK ISLAND EXPRESS. "MY GOD! THE
RAILS MOVE"—DEATH OF A BRAVE EN-
GINEER—A HELLISH CRIME—
$25,000 SECURFD—$50,000
REWARD—A VAIN OFFER

For some time previous to the Ste. Genevieve
bank robbery, the James brothers had seriously considered the question of enlarging their field of
operations. Bank plundering was all well enough
in its way. It was an easy, pleasant mode of giving them pocket money, but their aspirations
yearned for nobler deeds. The excitement of robbing banks was beginning to lose its pungency and
flavor. Their ambitions soared to greater latitudes,
and they had their hearts set on greater deeds.

To this end, Frank James and Bill Younger had
made a preliminary trip into Nebraska. A journey
of observation as it were, and, when they returned
and the conclave of marauders were once more in
session, they made their report. It was then determined to embark in the new enterprise. The
bankers had voted to change their business and

enter the wider field of railroading. In short, to rob express trains.

Two new men had been added to the gang. Robert Moore, and a Texas desperado who had flourished under the euphoneous cognomen of Comanche Toney. The conference was held in Jackson County, and with maps of the country, time tables and other printed and illustrated material, the question was viewed in all its possible and impossible phases.

There is considerable difference between holding up an express train, thundering along at forty miles an hour, and mulcting the bank in some sleepy little town of a few thousand frightened people. Besides, the idea was a new one. They were about to tread upon unknown ground, and they felt their way carefully. Various were the schemes proposed and rejected, and the discussion waxed warm. At length a decision was made, and, on the night of Saturday, July 20th, 1873, the James boys Jesse and Frank, Cole and Bill Younger, Bob Moore and Comanche Toney met at the rendezvous, a point on the Chicago, Rock Island & Pacific R. R. some fourteen miles from Council Bluffs.

The place had been selected with admirable forethought. A wild lonely country, half way between Adair and Des Moines, with not a single house for miles around. The east bound express was due there at about three o'clock in the morning, and it was this train they were to rob.

With commendable energy, the train robbers set to work. Spikes and fishplates were loosened, several ties were brought close at hand, ready for instant services, and then the men crept back to the bushes and waited: waited through the long night.

They waited and watched freight trains lumber safely over the loosened rails, which were still held by just enough spikes to keep them in place. They watched and waited until the East began to show signs of breaking of the Sabbath morn. At length the time for action drew near. Far down the track, the faint rumble of the approaching express was heard. Then the faint flash of the head light. Quickly the remaining spikes were drawn, and the rails thrust aside. The ties were thrown across the road bed just as the train, flying to make up time, crossed the Turkey Creek bridge. With bated breath, the hell inspired robbers watched the doomed express rushing to its destruction.

In the cab, poor John Rafferty, the engineer, peered ahead, his hand on the throttle. He saw the danger, but with a leap the engine struck the obstruction.

"My God, the rails move" cried Rafferty to his fireman.

It was his death cry, but even in the face of his awful peril, he thought of the passengers behind, and applying the air brake, he thrust back his lever.

With a hiss of steam, and a roar almost human in its agony, the engine sprang from the rails, and plunging to one side, fell over, crushing the life from the body of John Rafferty.

A cry of horror arose from the terrified passengers, and the cry was echoed by the wild yells of the damnable gang that had committed this hellish crime.

With curses and yells, the desperadoes ran through the cars, firing their revolvers, and commanding abject submission.

The express car was broken into and the messenger, with his arm broken by the bloodthirsty demons, was compelled to open the safe. The mail clerks were robbed, and then the ruthless villains passed through the cars, making every man, woman and child deliver their valuables. When the last passenger had been despoiled, the masked robbers disappeared in the bushes, mounted their horses, and rode gaily away, $25,000 richer, leaving the crushed and mangled body of the heroic John Rafferty, stretched out stiff in death, the rifled express car and the terror stricken passengers behind.

A reward of $50,000, was offered for the arrest of the robbers, but it was offered in vain. The villains escaped to Clay County and for a time disappeared.

CHAPTER XV

The Jesse James gang had never been afflicted with any great amount of modesty or bashfulness. The contrary was nearer the truth, and the success of their first venture in railroad robbery, emboldened them to even greater audacity. The money they secured from the Rock Island Express raid, enabled them to live without resort to any plundering expedition for a time, but one day, it was the middle of January, of 1884, five of the gang, Jesse and Frank James, Cole and Jim Younger and Cove Miller, by way of diversion, and to keep their hand in training, concluded to indulge in the pleasant task of robbing a stage.

Hot Springs was a great resort for invalids, troubled with rheumatism, paralysis and other ailments of that order, and, as the cost of living in Hot Springs was rather more than common, only the wealthy could patronize the place. A stage ran from Malvern, on the St. L. I. M. & S. R. R. to Hot Springs.

93

This morning, the stage was well filled, and had reached a point within five miles of the Springs, near the old Gaines mansion. The company in the stage were feeling in the best of good spirits, and were thoroughly enjoying the ride, when suddenly, five men, dressed in the uniform of Union soldiers, sprang from the bushes beside the road, each man carrying two revolvers.

"Stop, Stop!" cried one of the men, calling to the driver; "Stop, or I'll blow your head off."

The driver stopped. He didn't care to have his thatch blown skyward, and instantly reined in his horses.

"Come now, tumble out of here," was the next command, emphasized by a comprehensive movement of the pistols.

"Oh, certainly," responded one of the passengers a Mr. Charles Morse. "We can do nothing else."

The stage was soon vacant, save one old gentleman, who exclaimed piteously:

"I am paralyzed in my legs, and cannot walk."

"Never mind, then," said Jesse James, "stay where you are."

The other passengers, intimidated by the appearance of the dangerous looking revolvers of the men, did as they were told, and were formed in a circle, with their hands extended full arms length above their heads.

The robbers then began, systematically, to rob every man of the party. From Ex-Gov. Burbank

they took $800.00 in cash, a diamond pin worth
$350.00, and a gold watch valued at $250.00.
John Dietrich, of Little Rock, yielded up $200.00.
William Taylor, of Lowell, Mass., handed over
$650,00. Chas. Morse presented them with $70.00,
from E. A. Peebles of Hot Springs they took $200.00,
and Geo. E. Crump, of Memphis, turned over
$45.00. Other passengers gave $205.00, and the
Southern Express Company was robbed of $450.00.
A total of $3020.00, was secured by the five
robbers.

Somewhat jubilant over their success, and
secure in the knowledge that none of the passengers were armed, the brigands, in a facetious mood,
began to make coarse remarks, and indulge in a
species of grim humor, which they were pleased to
call pleasantries. The passengers, already badly
frightened, were thrown into a condition of actual
terror, by the outrageous actions of the robbers.

"I will bet you the pile," said Frank James to
Cole Younger, "that I can pink that chap on the
ear at fifty paces, nine times out of ten."

"Done." cried Younger. "but I can beat that."

"I must shoot first, though." continued Frank.

"D—d if you do." expostulated Younger. "I don't
want a dead man for a target."

The object of this wrangle, pale from fright, and
trembling with terror, begged his captors not to
use him as a target to test their skill at arms, and
begged that they would spare his life.

One of the passengers, Geo. W. Crump of Memphis, in answer to a question from Jesse, said he had been a soldier, and fought all through the war.

"On which side?" inquired the inquisitive Jesse.

"Confederate, of course." was the cunning reply.

"Well, d—n it all, your the right sort. We don't rob Confederate soldiers. Here's your wad. You're a brick.

Gov. Burbank, who had some valuable private papers in the pocket book stolen from him, begged that they would be returned to him on the ground that they were worthless to the robbers, but invaluable to him. Examining the papers, Jesse James thought they indicated that the Governor was a detective in disguise, and it would have gone hard with that gentleman, had he not succeeded in convincing the suspicious outlaws that he was no detective. The papers were returned and he was permitted to go.

For some time this cruel banter was kept up, until at last, wearied with their sport, the robbers prepared to depart. Frank James saluting the robbed passengers with mock politeness, and wishing them all a very good day, and another meeting, disappeared with his companions.

The plundered party reached Hot Springs without a cent on their persons, and although they received substantial aid from people in the hotel, and a plentiful supply of sympathy, the robbers were not pursued, and escaped scot free.

CHAPTER XVI

THE GADSHILL TRAIN RAID—STOPPED BY THE DANGER
SIGNAL. $12,000 TAKEN FROM THE ST. LOUIS AND
TEXAS EXPRESS—A SIXTY-MILE RIDE—THE
BOOTLESS PURSUIT—ESCAPED AGAIN

A month had not passed and Jesse James was at work again. But two short weeks after the Hot Springs stage-coach robbery, and a train was held up and plundered. The scene of operations selected by the train robbers, was the lonely station of Gadshill, on the Iron Mountain road, seven or eight miles from Piedmont. It was a cold, wintry day, the last day of January, about three o'clock in the afternoon, that a company of seven well mounted, heavily armed men, rode up to the flag station.

The town consisted of the station, a blacksmith shop, and a small store. The inhabitants were soon corralled, and stowed away in the station with strict injunctions to remain quiet. The train to be robbed was the St. Louis and Texas Express, which was due at 5.40 P. M. It was in charge of C. A. Alford, the conductor, and there were on board a large number of passengers and some valuable express freight.

As the train drew near Gadshill, the engineer saw the danger-signal displayed, and immediately brought the train to a standstill. No one was seen

Jesse James and his Band 7

upon the platform, but no sooner was the engine
at rest, than Cole Younger climbed aboard, and, at
the point of the pistol, drove the engineer and
fireman to the ground, where he kept them during
the entire period occupied in robbing the train.

Mr. Alford, the conductor, stepped from the car
to the platform to see what passengers were coming
aboard, and was met with the courteous request to
give up his money and watch and be "d—d quick
about it."

After giving up $50.00 and his watch, he was
put in the little station house.

With the train entirely in their own hands, the
robbers went through the cars in their usual manner, terrorizing and robbing the passengers.

It seemed incredible that a few men could
successfully hold an entire train load of people in
abject fear and trembling for any length of time,
and plunder them of their money and valuables
without meeting with some resistance, but, it is
one thing to talk of bravery and fight, hundreds of
miles away from the danger, and another thing to
be brave and fight in the presence of the same
dangers.

Imagine yourself curled up comfortably in your
seat, reading, or gazing dreamily from the car
window. You have been traveling some hundreds
of miles, and have settled into that lazy passiveness
which comes over one after listening for hours to
the monotonous singing of the rails, and whirr of

the wheels. The train slacks up, then stops. Nothing unusual in that you think, it is merely making its customary stop at some station; but, suddenly the doors at each end of the car are thrown open, and instead of the familiar form of the brakeman, you see a burly figure, roughly dressed, with a mask of some material over his face and two ugly revolvers stretched out before him. You suddenly awaken to the fact that it is business. You hear the rough, coarse tones of threatenings and oaths, as the figure advances into the car, and the stern voice commanding you, under pain of instant death, to hold up your hands, keep still, and keep your mouth shut. What will you do? You know there is another such man behind you, coming through the other door, you can hear his voice repeating the same terrible threatenings. Suppose you are a brave man, with a revolver in your pocket. Will you draw it? Will you make a single motion in that direction? Will you jeapordize the lives of yourself and fellow passengers, by any attempt? How do you know but what the keen, eager eyes of that strange figure, are upon you?

Indeed, you will do what is always done, you will keep still, with your two hands up in the air above your head, and you will shell out every cent you have and be thankful you escaped so easily. Besides you don't know but what there are a dozen such men behind you. You dare not turn your head to investigate. Curiosity is at a very low discount, when your life is to pay for it. It is the dread of the unknown that keeps you in your seat, passive and quiet.

It was just such sentiments and impulses that actuated every person on this particular train, and the James gang met no resistance, no hindrance in their collecting toll. The express and mail cars were plundered, and, with the booty obtained from the passengers, the robbers secured about $12.000

When their work was fully completed, the engineer and fireman were released, Mr. Alford, the conductor set at liberty and the train proceeded on its way.

The train-robbers mounted their horses, nor did they draw rein or stop, until sixty, good, long miles stretched between them and the scene of their exploit.

Armed men were at once sent in pursuit, and the telegraph was utilized in all directions, but, it was like chasing the north wind. So rapidly did the bandits ride, and so thorough was their geographical knowledge of the country, that pursuit was always a vain and bootless attempt.

Besides, it took brave men to hunt these desperadoes, and the paltry rewards offered for their apprehension was no inducement for a man to take his life in his hand, and proceed against such desperate men and unerring shots as Jesse James, or Cole Younger.

Thus they escaped again, and the world at large

laughed the officials to scorn, and held the state of
Missouri up to ridicule for the lack of energy displayed by the police department.

But the world at large, was not personally
acquainted with Jesse James, or the laugh would
have been on the other side of the mouth.

CHAPTER XVII

A COTERIE OF PLUNDERERS. JESSE JAMES' CONFEDERA-
TION OF BRIGANDS—WHO COMPOSED IT?—A FRATER-
NITY OF CUT-THROATS—RECKLESS DARE-DEVILS
—ORGANIZED RAID AGAINST THE FREE-
BOOTERS—A DUEL TO DEATH—JOHN
YOUNGER CAPT. LULL AND DE-
TECTIVE DANIELS KILLED

By this time, it had become clear to the most
obtuse observer of events, that there was a well-
organized *coterie* of lawless men who were banded
together for the single purpose of plunder. The
succession of bank robberies, stage plunderings and
train raidings were all executed by the same
persons. The success which formed such an important factor in the affairs, was due to deep laid
plans, exhaustive investigations, and splendid
executive ability.

The same characteristics were exhibited in every
crime and the *modus operandi* was uniform in all
events. In fact, the *coterie*, which was responsible for Russellville, Gallatin and Corydon, was responsible for the Gadshill raid, and the Gaines
Place stage robbery. It was Jesse James and his
band of notorious outlaws.

Such a confederacy of men had never before
existed. Crimes of such magnitude, perpetrated

with such unheard of impudence and audacity, had never before been conceived of. It was a unique organization, and commanded by a wonderful person, who stamped his individuality upon every raid, and left his trade-mark on every exploit.

Jesse James had plenty of material which he could utilize at any time. He had but to issue the word, and men came. Daring, bold, unscrupulous, heartless, cold blooded cut throats, who, with reckless disregard for their lives, would obey his slightest behest.

He was the leader, the executive head, but his brother Frank, crafty and shrewd, was the brainy man of the gang. It was he that did the planning, laid out the details, and did the scheming, but Jesse was the hand that executed. Then there was Cole and Jim Younger, second only to the James brothers in their particular line of work. George Sheperd was a desperado of the boldest type, and Sid Wallace, another wild freebooter, was often with the gang, Brad Collins and Jack Chunk were two Texans whose names were synonyms for bloodthirsty crimes throughout Texas and the West, and, with these were Tom Taylor, Clell Miller, Jim Cummings, Jim Anderson, Sam Bass, Bill Longley —a desperate character, Cal Carter, Jim Reed, and others of like stripe, who were always proud and anxious to get on a raid, or rob a bank with the James boys.

It was a fraternity of cut-throats, who hesitated at nothing—absolutely nothing, when engaged in any criminal adventure.

With this confederacy of crime existing, this band of bandits ranging Missouri, Kentucky, Iowa, Kansas, Arkansas and Texas, dashing here and there, pillaging, murdering, wrecking trains, robbing banks, carrying destruction wherever they went, the entire West was constantly in a state of apprehension. No man felt safe, no home was secure, no laws strong enough, no towns had sufficient protection from these reckless dare-devils.

The entire community became at last thoroughly aroused, and the Governors of Missouri and Arkansas offered large rewards, and the Express companies, who had suffered, together with the railroads, augmented these rewards for the arrest or death of any or all of the Jesse James band. Even the United States authorities, through the Post Office department, took a hand in the agitation, and determined, concerted action was agreed upon.

Allan Pinkerton, the noted detective, was brought into requisiton, and the Secret Service of the United States was ordered to co-operate with him.

With this vast machinery set in motion, all aiming for the destruction of the marauders, success seemed certain.

After several consultations, it was concluded best to send out several parties of men after the

outlaws. Each party or posse, working individu-
ally, but all combining in the good work of exter-
minating these murderous robber-pests. It was
hoped by a simultaneous movement of several
squads, that the bandits would become demoralized,
and, fleeing from one set of searchers, run into the
arms of another.

It was known too, that the gang had separated
after the Gadshill affair, although probably in
communication with each other.

The company that set out in search of the Younger
brothers, consisted of the entire detective force of
St. Clair County, commanded by one of Pinkerton's
best men; Capt. W. J. Allen, whose real name,
however was Lull. They had for their guides, Ed.
Daniels, of Osceola, and a St. Louis detective,
named Wright.

On the morning of March 16th, 1874, these three
men were out on a little expedition in advance of
the main body, and their journey brought them
near the home of a man named Theodoric Snuffer,
a great friend of the Younger brothers. At the
time, both John and James Younger were concealed
in the house, and observing the approaching trio of
horsemen, immediately comprehended their object.
Arming themselves with shot-guns, the desperadoes
slipped from the house, and making a slight detour,
suddenly appeared behind the men. Wright had
ridden some distance ahead, so it was two against
two.

Approaching from the rear, John Younger shouted.
"Halt, you d—d detectives. Hold up your hands!"
at the same time both brothers leveled their guns.
"Now, d—n you" continued Younger, "drop your
guns, or we'll kill you."

The bandits had the drop on them, so the detectives flung their pistol belts in the road.

Jim Younger picked up the pistols, while his
brother kept his gun on the detectives; but by a
fatal carelessness, lowered the barrel a second.
Quick as flash, Captain Lull shot from a revolver
he had concealed in his pocket, and John Younger
fell, with a ball through his throat; and the
carotid artery severed. In an instant, however, he
was up again, and fired the full charge of his gun
into Captain Lull, and both the desperado and
detective fell dead the same second.

Daniels, who also had a concealed revolver, fired
upon Jim Younger, wounding him slightly. The
latter, thrown into the wildest rage by the death of
his brother, rushed upon Daniels with the ferocity
of a maniac, but the detective fled to the woods.
Before he had reached the timber, Younger had
drawn on him, and sent him headlong from his
horse, with a bullet through the heart. Wright
saved himself by flight.

This tragic affair terminated the search for the
Younger brothers, for Jim fled from that section of
the country, swearing vengeance upon the entire
detective force of the country.

CHAPTER XVIII

Contemporaneous with the event which terminated so tragically with the death of John Younger, Captain Lull and Daniels, another drama was enacted in Clay County.

It was suspected that not only the James brothers, but others of the gang, were secreted in the vicinity of Kearney. In fact, certain and reliable information came to the authorities, that Jesse and Frank James were hid in the Samuels homestead.

When the news reached the Pinkertons in Chicago, it was deemed best to send some man to Kearney and endeavor to corral the entire lot of bush-rangers. Pinkerton had come to the conclusion that open, cross-country hunting would fail when such dashing, speedy game as the James brothers was to be chased. The mere fact that a posse of men were on horseback, would be of enough importance for some friend of the bandits to send warning.

Clay county was full of men who stood in with the audacious freebooters, either from motives of policy, sympathy, or friendship; and, with all the speed of the fastest horses, information and warning of impending danger would be sent to Jesse or Frank James in time for them to take the necessary measure for defence or flight.

With such overwhelming odds against them, the authorities were practically helpless.

Hence, Mr. Pinkerton determined to put his detective skill and cunning against the bold fearlessness of the outlaws, and the ready aid of their adherents.

John W. Wicher, a Chicago detective, one of Pinkerton's best men, volunteered for this hazardous duty. Although a young man, he was possessed of all the attriubtes which go to make up a first class detective. He was cool, collected, alert, flexible and brave. Over all, he was ambitious, and success, in such a proceeding as he contemplated, meant renown, money, and assured future prosperity.

Yet so perilous and dangerous was this projected movement, that Mr. Pinkerton deliberated some time before he finally allowed Wicher to depart.

The young detective had some plan of his own, and he was allowed to follow it, if he saw it was expedient.

Leaving Chicago early in March, he went directly to Liberty, the county seat of Clay County, and, while there, called on Mr. Adkins, the president of the Commercial Savings Bank.

This was a fatal error on his part, for Liberty was but a small place, and a stranger was a conspicuous object. Wicher was spotted at once by Jim Latche, who deemed it of enough importance to keep a wary eye on the young man. He saw Wicher leave the bank, and go to the home of ex-Sheriff Moss.

The detective had called on Col. Moss for information. He received it, but it was accompanied by an earnest plea from the ex-sheriff to abandon the hunt at once. The Colonel told the Chicago sleuth some terrible tales of Jesse James, pointed out to the daring detective the fearful risks he was taking in thus daring to beard the lion in his den, but, to all these friendly pleadings, Wicher turned a deaf ear. He had put his hand to the plow and would not turn back now. It was do or die. He did and died. Leaving the apprehensive Colonel, Wicher went to a convenient place and assumed the disguise of a tramp. Jim Latche saw him doing this, and the detective was a doomed man.

Mounting his horse, the outlaw sped to Kearney and before Wicher had scarcely left Liberty, Jesse James knew he was coming.

With Jesse James, were Jim Anderson and Brad Collins. Resolving on their plan of action, they moved toward Kearney, until removed a half mile from the Samuels homestead, and here they awaited the young detective.

Wicher reached Kearney in the afternoon, and, without a moment's hesitation, proceeded directly for the house of Dr. Samuels.

He was passing up the road, when suddenly he was confronted by the three waiting outlaws. Somewhat astonished, but perfectly cool, Wicher said:

"Good evening."

"Where in hell are you going?" was the brutal answer.

"I'm hunting for a job. Can you tell me where I can get one?"

"Not by a d—d sight. Old Pinkerton has given you a job that will last you as long as you care to live, I reckon."

This crushing reply told Wicher that it was all up with him, and he knew his hours were numbered, when Jesse James drew his revolver and waved it maliciously before him. But Wicher was plucky and he made one more attempt.

"What do you mean?" he said, "I tell you I'm hunting for a job. I don't know Pinkerton, or any of his crowd, and I haven't time to fool with you for I've got to get a place to sleep tonight."

At this, Jesse James laughed outright.

"You won't want to sleep anywhere tonight, young man, your little game is known. What did you deposit money at Liberty for? What do you want with Adkins and Moss? Where are your own clothes? You d—d fool, do you think you are smart enough to come around here and play some of your smart Pinkerton tricks; you can just say you killed yourself, for you're going to be killed. Come, move on!"

The detective was immediately disarmed, bound with a cord, and a gag put in his mouth.

"Damned fine hands for a laboring man," said one of the outlaws, pointing to Wicher's soft palms.

"The dirty liar ought to die."

When evening had fairly set in, Wicher was placed on a horse, and guarded by Jesse James, Jim Anderson and Brad Collins, was taken from the place where they had concealed him, and the terrible procession moved toward the Blue Hills. For hours they rode.

The mental agony which racked the brain of the young detective, can only be imagined. He was a young husband. He had but kissed his wife farewell a few days before, full of hope, life and ambition. Tonight, he was a doomed man, led to his execution. Through the country he was taken, every step, every second bringing him nearer his death. Death, far from his loved ones, death by violence, death as a reward for doing his duty.

The stern, gloomy, pitiless faces of his self-appointed executioners, peered at him through the dusk, and the hoofs of their shadowy horses beat the cadence of the death march; terrible, agonizing music for the man who was to die.

At last the appointed spot was reached, and poor Wicher, pulled roughly from the horse, was tied to a tree.

He was relieved of the gag, and then the hellish brutes began a torture which would have shamed the wild Indian of Arizona. Refusing to divulge any information concerning Pinkerton, he was slashed with their keen knives until his body was covered with cuts. His head was twisted until the neck was nearly broken. He was subjected to indignities which must have been invented by a fiend from hell; and then, when the brutal monsters had grown weary, two bullets, merciful missiles, sped through his heart and brain, and the young detective was dead! With a jest and a curse, the three murderers leaped to their horses, and rode home to breakfast.

A young wife in Chicago, that morning wrote a letter to her dear husband. She knew he would love to read a word from her. But the husband was a mutilated corpse; ghastly and horrid in its disfigurement, stark and stiff in death, and thrown across a country road, far down in Jackson County; left there by Jesse James as a warning; and the young wife, singing, that lovely March morning, busy with her household cares, was a widow.

And thus ended the tragedy of Wicher the detective.

CHAPTER XIX

PINKERTON'S STERN RESOLVE—"EXTERMINATE THE EN-
TIRE BROOD"—SAMUELS' HOUSE UNDER WATCH AND
WARD. THE ASSAULT ON CASTLE JAMES. A
DASTARDLY DEED—CHILDREN SLAUGHTERED
BY HAND-GRENADES—MRS. SAMUELS
SERIOUSLY WOUNDED—MISERABLE
FAILURE OF THE ATTACK

When the news came to Pinkerton that Wicher
had been murdered, and that Lull and Daniels had
been sacrificed in ridding the world of John
Younger, the department was agitated by conflicting
emotions of the most poignant nature. Sorrow and
grief for the untimely death of the detectives, indignation and anger against the murderers for the
inhuman butchery of Wicher, chagrin and mortifi-
cation for the failures. The skill and finesse of
the detective association had been absolutely without virtue. Cunning had been overcome by brute
force; craftiness by murder, and the inhuman world
laughed and held Pinkerton up to undeserved
scorn.

All of this spurred him to renewed efforts, and it
was determined to commence a campaign against
the Jesse James gang, which would either exterminate it, or drive it from the country. No half way
measures were to be tolerated, no mercy was to be

shown. The entire brood was to be swept from Missouri.

William Pinkerton, with five of his best men, located in Kansas City, and at once sent for the sheriff of Clay county. When that gentleman came, the plans for the campaign were thoroughly settled, and every bit of detail in the matter of exigencies was provided for. Nothing was to be left for chance.

A strict and sleepless watch was put upon the Samuels' home, and trusty citizens, who were willing to risk their lives in ridding Clay County of the outlaws, and cleansing the community from the approbrium that rested upon it, were employed to keep watch and ward in all sections of the country.

One afternoon, both Frank and Jesse James were seen in the yard before Dr. Samuels' house. A report to that effect was forwarded to Kearney, and thence to Kansas City.

The time had come to strike the decisive blow, and Mr. Pinkerton gave the order to move on to the enemy's works. The day was January, 25th, 1875. and at midnight, a strong posse of citizens, detec tives, and police officers quietly surrounded the house. They were well armed and provided with fire balls made of tow, saturated with kerosene oil, and two hand-grenades of the most explosive pattern.

Just at midnight, nine of Pinkerton's best men, stepped forward to make the first assault on "Castle

James." Two of them approached a side window to investigate, and in so doing, awoke a colored woman, who immediately gave the alarm. Hastily breaking the window, the flaming fire balls were tossed into the room, and the attacking cordon of men, their guns and revolvers ready, waited in breathless suspense for the appearance of the two desperadoes, ready to shoot them down without mercy, should they come out. But, though the fire and smoke drove Dr. Samuels and his wife, Susie Samuels, and the childern to the rooms below, no Jesse or Frank James appeared.

Then occurred a dastardly piece of business. Overcome by the excitement, one of the detectives hurled a hand-grenade into the midst of the women and children, who were huddled together, filled with consternation and terror. An explosion followed, and from the smoke of the bursted shell, came screams of anguish, and shrieks of pain. But, the brigands, the outlaws, the James brothers, made no sign. They were fifty miles away, securely housed in the home of a friend, safe from harm.

It was a cowardly act, this throwing of the hand grenade. It was entirely inexcusable, and can never be justified. When the smoke had cleared away, the little eight-year-old son of Mrs. Samuels was writhing in the agonies of death, his entire side torn away by the explosive. Mrs. Samuels lay on the floor, her left arm shattered, and hanging at her side. Susie and an old servant, were covered with blood and wounds, and blood was spattered everywhere.

The assaulting party were paralyzed at the sight, and silently left the scene, just as the little boy, with a scream of anguish, turned on his side and expired.

If Jesse or Frank James had been present, the results would have been different. The assaulters would have left some of their number dead on the ground, but, the carefully planned attack ended in the wanton slaughter of an innocent, and the James brothers were still alive and free.

Several years after, Mrs. Samuels was asked if Jesse or Frank were home that night.

With a stern, contemptuous gaze, the old woman answered: "Home? And do you think that if either of my boys had been home, that those men would have escaped. There would have been a dozen dead detectives if my sons had been present." And she probably told the truth.

CHAPTER XX

The terrible tragedy at Kearney, that 25th of
January, was followed by the funeral of the boy
that was killed. It was attended by the entire
country. The tide of sympathy, by one of those
curious incongruities of life, had turned in favor of
the James boys. No matter what people thought
of them, no matter how guilty they were, the wanton slaughter of the innocent, the detestable
cowardice exhibited in casting an explosive bomb
into a crowd of women and children, created a
revulsion of feeling, and the detectives were bit-
terly condemned and denounced.

Indeed, the matter was taken up by the State
Legislature of Missouri, and Gen. Jeff Jones, a
member from Callaway County, introduced the
following remarkable measure, and championed it
by a most eloquent speech.

The following quotations will serve to indicate
the purport and intent of the "Outlaw Amnesty
Bill:"

WHEREAS, By the 4th section of the
11th Article of the Constitution of Missouri, all persons in the military service
of the United States, or who acted under
the authority thereof in this state, are relieved from all civil liability and all
criminal punishment for all acts done by
them since the 1st day of January, A. D.
1861: and,

WHEREAS, By the 12th section of the said
11th Article of said Constitution provision
is made by which, under certain circumstances, may be seized, transported to,
indicted, tried and punished in distant
counties, any Confederate under ban of
despotic displeasure, thereby contravening
the Constitution of the United States and
every principle of enlightened humanity;
and,

WHEREAS, Such discrimination evinces
a want of manly generosity and statesmanship on the part of the party imposing,
and of courage and manhood on the part of
the party submitting tamely thereto; and,

WHEREAS, Under the outlawry pro-
nounced against Jesse W. James, Frank
James, Coleman Younger, Robert Younger
and others, who gallantly periled their
lives and their all in defense of their
principles, they are of necessity made

desperate, driven as they are from the fields of honest industry, from their friends, their families, their homes and their country, they can know no law but the law of self-preservation, nor can have no respect for and feel no allegiance to a government which forces them to the very acts it professes to deprecate, and then offers a bounty for their apprehension, and arms foreign mercenaries with power to capture and kill them; and,

WHEREAS, Believing these men too brave to be mean, too generous to be revengeful, and to gallant and honorable to betray a friend or break a promise; and believing further that most, if not all of the offences with which they are charged have been committed by others, and perhaps by those pretending to hunt them, or by their confederates; that their names are and have been used to divert suspicion from and thereby relieve the actual perpetrators; that the return of these men to their homes and friends would have the effect of greatly lessening crime in our state by turning public attention to real criminals, and that common justice, sound policy and true statesmanship, alike demand that amnesty should be extended to all alike of both parties for all acts done or charged

to have been done during the war; there-
fore, be it

*Resolved, By the House of Representatives,
the Senate concurring therein:*

That the Govenor of the State be, and he
is hereby requested to issue his proclamation notifying the said Jesse W. James,
Frank James, Coleman Younger, Robert
Younger, and James Younger, and others,
that full and complete amnesty and pardon
will be granted them for all acts charged
or committed by them during the late civil
war, and inviting them peacefully to
return to their respective homes in this
state and there quietly remain, submitting
themselves to such proceedings as may be
instituted against them by the courts for
all offences charged to have been committed since said war, promising and guaran-
teeing to them and each of them full protection and a fair trial therein, and that
full protection shall be given them from
the time of their entrance into the State and
his notice thereof under said proclamation
and invitation.

The bill was introduced in March of 1875, and
although ably supported, was defeated.

It is doubtful if the James brothers would have
accepted the conditions of this act. To have surrendered to the authorities, meant either imprison-

NORTHFIELD BANK RAID.

ment for life or death by hanging, and neither were
anxious to end their liberty or existence. They
had been outlawed with all due formality by Gov.
Silas Wordson, and this act of the Legislature
ratified the decree against them.

They were doubly outlawed. For them, there
was no mercy. Any man could shoot them down,
and receive a full pardon for the act.

They reorganized after this and, incited to further
acts of retaliation and revenge on account of the
tragedy at their home, they entered more com-
pletely than ever into the dark life they had been
leading, and resolved to do greater deeds and in-
spire greater fear.

When Jesse James learned of the fatal conse-
quences which attended the midnight attack on his
home, his rage and fury knew no bounds. Villainous and reckless as he was, his filial affection was
well known, and his family ties were strong. It
was this affection which induced himself and
brother Frank to take such risks in visiting his
mother's habitation, and the news of the little
brother's death was a great shock to this outlawed
murderer. At once he began investigating.
Searching for the men who were engaged in that
lamentable affair. Suspicion fell upon many, but
it pointed to none so strongly as it did to a Daniel
Askew, a flourishing farmer, whose land lay near
the Samuels house.

The utmost secrecy had been carefully main-

tained by the posse who threw the fire balls and
hand-grenade into the house that 25th, of January,
and the members of the party, moved by sentiments
of personal safety, took every precaution to keep
their share in the exploit from becoming known.

This Mr. Askew even disclaimed any connection
with the assaulting party. He reiterated again and
again, that he had done nothing whatever, and
knew absolutely nothing concerning the tragedy.

However, he fell under suspicion, and Jesse
James felt certain that Mr. Askew was not only one
of the party, but was a leader in the attack.

On the night of April 12th, following the attack
on Dr. Samuels' home; Mr. Askew, after his supper,
sauntered to a spring about two hundred feet from
his home to get a bucket of water.

The moon was full, and made the night bright
as day. He secured the water and had returned,
setting the bucket on the porch, when three shots
rang out, and the farmer fell dead, pierced with
three rifle-balls.

The wife and daughter, startled by the shots,
rushed from the kitchen in time to see three men
dart from a woodpile, mount their horses and ride
rapidly away, leaving the murdered farmer stretched out upon his own porch.

The three men whom Mrs. Askew saw riding
away were Jesse and Frank James, and their boon
friend, Clell Miller.

This murder again gave the fickle public an

opportunity to change its mind. Mr. Askew was a prominent man in the community, and his atrocious death filled the public mind with a sincere desire to rid the country of the James brothers and their lawless comrades.

It became too warm for the bandits, and they pulled up stakes, and sought fresh stamping grounds.

The members of the party were Jesse and Frank James, Clell Miller, Jim Reed, Cole and Jim Younger. Decamping from Missouri, they went to Indian Territory, and turned horse-thieves. Tiring of this innocent amusement, they set their faces southward and invaded Texas. The stage coach which ran between San Antonia and Austin tempted them, and they resolved to hold it up. Accordingly they laid their plans, and March 12th, 1875, found them in ambuscade on the stage road, twenty-five miles from Austin.

The passenger list on that eventful afternoon comprised eleven ladies and gentlemen, among whom were Bishop Gregg of the Episcopal Church, bishop in charge of the Diocese of Texas, and Mr. Breckenridge, President of the First National Bank of San Antonio.

The passengers had eaten their supper at a wayside station, and were bowling along rapidly toward their destination. In the midst of the genial flow of conversation, the driver discerned the figures of six mounted men, some little distance ahead of the coach, and took them to be rancheros. As they approached, however, he noticed that their horses were not the ungainly cow-ponies of the region, but fine animals of a thoroughbred air.

Apprehension filled his breast, and his fears were excited. His suspicions were soon realized, for, as he drew near them, the foremost horseman turned, and presenting a huge revolver, called out in tones of no uncertain sound:

"Halt d—n your soul, or I'll fill you so full of lead that some tenderfoot will locate you for a mineral claim."

The driver, with the discretion bred of experience, and the promptitude inspired by the business-like aspect of the threatening revolver, pulled in his horses, and brought the stage to an abrupt stand-still.

Immediately, the six brigands surrounded the vehicle, and a rough voice shouted out:

"Tumble out here now, lively. Come be quick, if you don't want to die where you sit."

Confusion reigned. The women threw themselves in the arms of the gentlemen, begging to be protected, and a fleshy female, whose avoirdupois was at an inverse ratio to her spirit, clung to the reverend bishop, beseeching him in the most heart-rending terms, to preserve her from harm; but the bishop was helpless in the matter. He had been ordered, in ungentle accents, by a rough highwayman behind a monster of a pistol, to "tumble out"; hence he tumbled.   Likewise the other gentlemen of the party, and they were ranged in two lines and guarded by a couple of the robbers, whilst the remainder of the outlaws broke open boxes, pried apart the baggage, and ransacked the stage.

The ladies were told that no harm was intended. They would not be molested, all they had to do was to keep quiet.

After pillaging the stage the robbers turned their attention to the personal belongings of the passengers.

The Bishop endeavored to escape the contribution box by pleading that he was a clergyman, but his auditors were not in a repentant mood, nor were they inclined to respect the cloth.   They took what he had and wanted more; twitting him by making facetious remarks concerning his calling, and even venturing to suggest sage advice for his future actions.   Mr. Breckenridge proved a bonanza, for from him, Jesse James took over $1,000.   The ladies surrendered their money and jewels, and in all they secured about $3,500.

After taking the head span of horses, they signified that they were through, and permitted the coach to proceed.

With this money the gang was able to live quite comfortably for a time, but "easy come—easy go," the gang became strapped again, and were ready for another stroke of business.   They decided to try railroading again, and soon had their plans laid for another raid.

CHAPTER XXII

Some time in December following the San Antonio
stage robbery, Jesse James obtained information
that the Government intended shipping a large
quanity of gold dust from Denver, via the Kansas
Pacific. Just how the wily bandits ascertained
this fact, is not known, but the presumption is that
he had a friend in "court" who kept him posted in
such financial transactions.

When he learned of the projected shipment, he
immediately called his band together, and the
council was held in Texas. As a result of their
deliberations, the coterie of train robbers moved
northward to Kansas. Just outside of Kansas City,
some six miles or so, is the little town of Muncie.
It is hardly more than a water tank on the Kansas

Pacific road, and is quite remote from any habitations.

This little, insignificant station was the objective point of the outlaws' journey, and here they rendezvoused Christmas day.

It was quite dark when the Express drew up to Muncie, and the fireman was about to spring up on top ot the tender to fix the water pipe, when a shrill whistle was heard, and a dark figure sprang from behind the tank, and into the cab.

Before the engineer could fairly comprehend what was up, Bill McDaniels, one of the James band, had leveled his revolver, and swore that he would shoot to kill, if either the engineer or fireman made a move. While McDaniels was thus intimidating the two men on the engine, the raiders were busy behind, in the cars.

Rushing through the train, they commanded instant surender and absolute quiet. This command backed up by pistols, was obeyed to the letter. Two men stood on each platform, guarding the train, while three of them rushed into the express car.

The messenger in charge was quickly overcome, and in fifteen minutes they had looted the car of $30,000 worth of gold dust, and $25,000 of silver and other valuables. Fifteen short, fleeting minutes was all the time required to rob the train of this enormous amount. Not a finger was raised to hinder them, not a word of protest was spoken.

After the car had been thoroughly ransacked, a shrill whistle again gave the command, and the robbers disappeared in the darkness.

$55,000! A clean, quick job. It was, to express the sentiments of a disgusted railroad official, a beautiful bit of work, but d—d expensive.

Some days after the robbery, Bill McDaniels, unable to stand prosperity, undertook to give Kansas City a strong coat of paint, of a rich cardinal hue, and, in course of events, was arrested for being drunk. On him was found a leather bag and a large sum of money, which he swore—when he finally sobered up—was honestly earned in Colorado

But suspicion was aroused, and the redoubtable William was removed to Lawrence, Kansas. To Lawrence, the unhappy town which once suffered by the hands of Quantrell. To Lawrence, which once trembled and bled when the "black flag" swept her streets, and now—poetic justice, Bill McDaniels, one of the guerillas that aided in striking the fair town so foul a blow, was sent there in chains.

A detective, a certain O'Hara, was detailed to pump McDaniels, but he did not possess enough suction ability, for the oyster-mouthed Bill refused to talk.

As the constables were taking him from the caboose for trial, the wily outlaw gave them the slip, and escaped to the woods. For a week he escaped capture, but succumbed to the fatal bullet from the rifle of a man named Bauerman, and fell,

9

a dying man. But even in death, he remained faithful to the gang, and died without divulging the slightest hint.

Rough, uncouth, treacherous villains were these marauders, but faithful to their pals, and it was their boast and wish, that they could die with their boots on, and die game.

It was probably this sentiment that enabled the dying bandit to keep sacred the oath he took; although he was subjected to a skillful sweating process in the vain hopes that . some information could be squeezed from him which would be of some value as throwing light on the Muncie train robbery.

The following April, West Virginia felt the hand of the James band. It is a long jump from Kansas City, Missouri, to Huntington, West Virginia, but, business is business, and such enterprising business men as the James brothers do not hesitate to take long business trips. Ah! no, it is a mere jaunt, and the bank of Huntington was doing such a neat, tidy little business, that it looked like a good investment. So the corporation of James Brothers sent Frank James, Cole Younger, Tom McDaniels—brother of Bill, heroic Bill, who kept his mouth shut, and earned everlasting fame in Missouri; and a gentleman of sporting proclivities, and keen insight into the peculiarities of . carrying balances, not in, but from banks, who came from Texas, by the name of Jack Keen, as a committee of four to investigate. This committee of distinguished citizens from Missouri, paid Huntington a visit, and Huntington, hospitable to a degree, felt that such visits were expensive, and hereafter, would rather be excused. Huntington considers $10,000 a visit somewhat luxurious in the matter of living.

Huntington is a cosy little town on the C. & O. R. R., and is situated on the Ohio river.

About two o'clock in the afternoon of this April day, the cashier of the bank received a call from the Missourians, who had meandered down the quiet street on horseback.

In the insinuating terms which have such persuasive eloquence when accompanied by a life like copy of a business-like revolver, Mr. James intimated that a loan of what ready cash the bank had on hand, would relieve him of a temporary embarrassment which was causing him much anxiety.

The cashier, Mr. Olney, only too glad to accomodate such distinguished gentlemen, threw the vault doors open, and allowed them to help themselves. They did—$10,000.

In an hour, the sheriff and twenty five citizens were after them, and the Missourians, feeling that they had been somewhat precipitate in their dealings with the bank, clapped spurs to their horses and fled.

They fled just four weeks. Twenty-eight days did those citizens of Huntington follow them.

Tom McDaniels intercepted a stray bullet, and was buried where he fell. Jack Keen was captured in Fentress County, Tennessee, and sent to the penitentiary for eight years, but Frank James and Cole Younger rode gaily on, and stopped not until they were in Indian Territory. They divided the $10,000 between themselves, $5,000 each; not so bad.

CHAPTER XXIII

Jesse James was not engaged in the Huntington raid in person, although he was present in spirit.

He met Frank, after the latter had at last eluded his persevering pursuers, in the Indian Territory.

Hardly had the brothers joined each other, when their active minds began to plan another raid upon the railroad companies, and they soon had a carefully prepared plot to rob an express train.

The James boys were now at the head of a large gang of desperadoes, desperate villains, in for any crime, and anxious to assume any risk, so the reward was ample enough. The McDaniels brothers, the Shepherd brothers, Bill Longley, and some of the old gang, had shuffled off their mortal coils, but there was still the Younger boys, Clell Miller, Sam Bass, Haskins and Moore, of Indian Territory, Hobbs Kerry, a Texas man, full of blow, brag, and buck courage, Bill Chadwell and Charlie Pitts.   These men comprised Jesse James' gang at this time.

The train selected was one on the Missouri Pacific, and the place was Rocky Cut, just where the huge bridge spans the Lamine River.   A watchman was constantly employed on this bridge, and his shanty was located at one of the terminals.

The plan to be carried into execution, was simple.   First, overpower the watchman, secure his red lantern, stop the train, rob it and ride away.   The date selected was July 8th, 1876.

By sun-down of this day, the entire party of train-robbers, had gathered at the bridge.

Stealthily approaching, they dismounted in a thick bed of foliage near the watchman's house, and, leaving Bill Chadwell and Hobbs Kerry to look after the nags, the rest of the band descended in force on the watchman.

Clell Miller, Charlie Pitts and Bob Younger easily induced the frightened man to give in, and secured the coveted red lantern.

In order to make assurance doubly sure, a few rails were loosened, ready to be torn from the ties, and some ties and rocks were heaped upon the road bed.   But fortunately, the obstructions were not required.   The train came along, the red light was waved, and soon the puffing engine stood at rest, and was immediately boarded by two of the robbers, who held their revolvers against the heads of the engineer and fireman. At the same time, the masked raiders swarmed on the cars and the passengers were apprised of the fact that the train was in the hands of professional robbers.

The leaders, Jesse and Frank James, Clell Miller and Bob Younger, at the points of their revolvers, compelled the express messenger to open the door of his car, and open the safe.

The booty, about $17,000, was tumbled into the leather sack, a shrill whistle warned the guards that the task was done, and the surrounding dark-ness swallowed up the entire band of marauders.

Mounting their horses, the robbers rode rap-idly from the scene, and, as usual, after divid-ing the spoils, separated, subject to call.

Hobbs Kerry, or Cub Kerry, as he was called by his familiars, gravitated to Fort Worth, Texas, and proceeded to blow himself out.

His flush appearance, and reckless expenditure of the ready cash, aroused suspicions, and the Cub was jailed. After lying in durance vile for a long time, he squealed, but he squealed too loudly. He squealed too long, and squealed too much. The consequence was, that he was not believed, and although he told all he knew about the Lamine Bridge affair, he told a great deal more than was necessary, and so the Cub's squealing did him no good nor the James brothers any harm.

Large rewards were offered for the train robbers, but then, this was always done after the train had been relieved of several thousand dollars. It is very easy to offer rewards, but another thing to earn them.

What though the entire detective and constabulary force of Missouri, Arkansas, Kansas and the Indian Territory was out and scouring the entire country, it was worse than hunting the proverbial needle in the proverbial hay stack. Then again, it was all very pleasant to hunt these men. It was like hunting the tiger. So long as you are hunting the tiger, it is all pleasant, agreeable sport, but when the tiger turns round and begins to hunt you, well—"

CHAPTER XXIV

BILL CHADWELL—JESSE JAMES CONCLUDES TO TRY MIN-
NESOTA—A CHOICE PARTY SELECTED—THE COUNCIL
OF WAR—NORTHFIELD, MINN., SELECTED—MEET-
ING AT MANKATO—STUDYING GEOGRAPHY—
SANGUINE HOPES OF THE RAIDERS
— COLE YOUNGER'S DARK
PRESENTIMENT.

Bill Chadwell, who had joined the Jesse James gang just before the Lamine Bridge affair, was a Minnesota horse-thief. In that country he was dreaded and feared as was Jesse James and Clell Miller in Missouri and Texas. He was a wild, dashing blade, cut on the same lines as the Missouri outlaws, and was wanted in Minnesota for numerous little horse-stealing affairs. He told Jesse and Frank James all about Minnesota, and pointed out to them the peculiar advantages that State offered for such business enterprises as the James brothers affected. Minnesota had been comparatively free from any such affairs, and Chadwell urged that an expedition into the wheat belt would be productive of great profits.

Jesse James was favorably disposed to make the attempt, and he made up a choice and select party for the occasion. He had another object in trying his luck in the Northern State. The police were

getting altogether too lively for comfort. The entire country of Missouri, Kansas, Arkansas and the
Indian Territory was under close surveilance, and
detectives were scouring and swarming everywhere.

By making a sudden dash to the North, the
police would be thrown off the track, and com-
pletely baffled.

A council was held, and the Minnesota man's
plans laid before the select party. This gang consisted of Jesse and Frank James, Cole, Jim and
Bob Younger, Charlie Pitts, Clell Miller and Bill
Chadwell. It was decided to move on to Northfield, a town in Rice County, on the C. M. & St.
P. R. R.

The Northfield bank was reputed to be a very
wealthy institution and offered great inducements to
the avaricious outlaws.

When all was arranged, the eight men separated,
and made their various ways to Mankato, where
the entire ground was gone over. The great factor, which had so much to do with the successful
issue of their various raids and robberies, was the
intimate acquaintance with the country which the
James brothers possessed. Every road, cross-road,
short-cut, lane, ford, creek, bridge, hill and gully in
Missouri were familiar objects to them. They
knew where they were and where they could go.
In the darkest nights, their swift horses would
bear them over rough countries which would
appall an ordinary horseman in broad daylight.

They made it a practice, never to make a move until the geography of the adjacent and surrounding country was mastered.

In this case, they were dependent on Bill Chadwell for guidance, but he knew Minnesota and Iowa as well as the James brothers knew Clay County, Missouri, or Charlie Pitts the Pan Handle of Texas.

Everything pointed to a successful raid. It was to be done as it had always been done. The same tactics were to be pursued, hence, the same results, hence, success.

With these sanguine hopes, the bank-raiders perfected their plans for robbing the Northfield bank. They were domiciled at the house of a friend of Chadwells, in Mankato, and made several trips to Northfield for the purpose of getting acquainted with the country, and familiar with the immediate surroundings. Cole Younger did not approve of this raid. Some premonition of disaster impelled him to urge another place. He said he would rather try Canada, Quebec or Toronto in preference to Northfield. But the matter was put to a final vote, and Northfield won. It was September 3rd, 1876, when the decision was made, and it was determined to make the attempt the following Thursday, September 6th.

CHAPTER XXV

NORTHFIELD, MINN.—THE FATAL SIXTH OF SEPTEMBER—
THREE STRANGE HORSEMEN—FIVE DEMONS TERRIFY
NORTHFIELD. "I'LL DO MY DUTY IF I DIE FOR
IT." T. L. HAYWOOD, CASHIER, MURDERED
—PANDEMONIUM REIGNS SUPREME—A
MEDICAL NIMROD—CHARLIE PITTS
KILLED—BILL CHADWELL SHOT
JIM YOUNGER WOUNDED
—A DISASTROUS FAIL-
URE—THE RIDE FOR
LIFE—RETRIBU-
TION PUR-
SUES

Northfield, itself, has a population of twenty-five hundred people. It is located in the north-eastern section of Rice County, on the line of Dakota County, and is, next to Faribault, one of the chief towns of Rice County. Surrounded on all sides by the rich wheat belt of Minnesota it was a thriving, prosperous city.

The farming community dependent on Northfield for supplies, was of that intelligent, progressive, sturdy stock that has placed Minnesota in the front ranks of statehood, and created an enlightened civilization that is the admiration of the country.

The Chicago, Milwaukee and St. Paul Railway passed through Northfield, and was an important factor in its progress and active condition.

About noon, on this fatal sixth of September,
three strange men on horse-back, came into Northfield, from the north, and ate their dinner in a
hotel on the other side of the river. They entered
freely into conversation, even wagering money on
the coming election. No one knew who they were
nor suspected them of any evil intentions, yet
these cool horsemen were Jesse James, Frank James
and Cole Younger. After a hearty dinner, the trio
mounted their horses, and rode leisurely toward
the bank, which was located in the prominent business block in the public square.

Dismounting, they tied their horses in front of
the bank, and remained on the sidewalk, conversing in a most ordinary manner for a few minutes,
then turned and entered the bank. As they did this,
three horsemen dashed across the bridge at full
speed, carrying revolvers in their hands. As soon
as they had entered the town, they commenced
shooting indiscriminately to the right and left,
shouting and yelling all manner of threats. At the
same moment two other mounted men appeared
from the west, yelling like demons and firing
their pistols, commanding the people to remain
in their houses. When the five men met before the
bank, they faced in different directions and flourishing their revolvers, swore to kill instantly, any
man who dared approach them.

Meantime, the three outlaws who had entered the
bank were engaged in committing a most dastardly

murder. The cashier, Mr. J. L. Haywood, glanced up as the men passed through the door, and was confronted by a large revolver. Without a moment's hesitation the three robbers sprang over the counter and Frank James, drawing his knife, held it at the cashier's throat, and ordered him to open the safe.

Nothing daunted by his perilous position, the courageous man said:

"I will do no such thing."

"Quick now." commanded Jesse James, placing his revolver at Mr. Haywood's head, "or you die like a dog."

"I can't help that!" was the brave reply. "I'll do my duty if I die for it."

"Then G—d d—n you, die!" said Jesse and he pulled the trigger.

Poor Haywood dropped dead at his murderer's feet.

Cole Younger then turned to the assistant cashier, Mr. A. E. Bunker.

"Come here, d—n you, and open this safe!"

Bunker disclaimed all knowledge of the combination, and with a wild dash, gained the back door. As he was escaping, Younger fired, and Mr. Bunker received the bullet in his shoulder. He escaped without further damage. The junior clerk, Frank Wilcox, slipped away without molestation.

While the baffled murderers were making a vain search for the money-box, retribution had overtaken their comrades outside.

Dr. Wheeler, a plucky physician, who occupied rooms opposite the bank, heard the commotion, and, looking through the windows, saw the entire proceedings. Picking up a shot gun, he took deliberate aim, and sent the entire charge of shot into the heart of Charlie Pitts, who gave one wild yell, crying as he threw up his arms, and fell from his plunging horse:

"My God! Boys, I'm done for!"

Again the Doctor fired, and Bill Chadwell, the notorious and dreaded horse-thief of Minnesota, fell in mortal agony upon the ground.

By this time, others had joined in the fray. A. K. Manning, Joseph Hyde, and George Betts obtained guns, and began firing. Another outlaw dropped and his horse ran away, but Clell Miller, dashing forward, threw the wounded man across the saddle—it was Jim Younger--and fled for his life.

In the midst of the melee, Jesse and Frank James, and Cole Younger ran from the bank. They did not find the money, and now it was a matter of life or death.

Quickly mounting their horses, they fled, firing right and left.

Bill Chadwell and Charlie Pitts lay dead before the bank doors. Jim Younger, fearfully wounded, was carried by Clell Miller; and Jesse James, Frank James, Cole Younger and Bob Younger were fleeing for their very lives, before the furious citizens of Northfield, who, mad with excitement, and at a white heat for vengeance, had instantly set out in pursuit of the blood-thirsty villians who had so wantonly murdered Mr. Haywood.

The telegraph sped the news on all sides, and pursuing parties sprang up in every direction. Retribution was swiftly following the flying brigands. The avenger of blood was hot on their trail. Disaster, like a dark cloud hovered over them, threatening every instant to engulf them in its deadly folds.

On and on they sped. Faster and faster they flew, but swifter than their fleet steeds, Justice followed, and the bank-robbers could almost see the flash of her terrible sword. It was a fatal, dreadful day for them. Defeat and disaster, death and wounds, flight and capture were theirs instead of booty. Truly the ways of the transgressor is hard.

CHAPTER XXVI

Before Jesse James and his comrades had fairly got out of town, fifty men, earnest, determined citizens of Northfield, were in the saddle and in furious pursuit of the bandits.

The news of the murder had been telegraphed far and near. Every town in Minnesota, Iowa and Dakota had complete descriptions of the murderers, of their horses and clothing, and before twenty-four hours had elapsed, four hundred men were searching for six.

Sentinels and guards were posted at every bridge and ford, every road had its vigilant watchers, waiting for these terrible six men to come along. Every town was on the *qui vive*, and every man in Minnesota, constituted himself a posse of one to

Jesse James and His Band 10

help hunt down the dastards and scoundrels who had killed a brave man.

The news reached St. Paul, and Gov. Pillsbury at once offered a reward of $1,000 for each robber or $6,000 for the gang. Then began a hunt to the death.

Four hundred hunters against six hunted.

Beset on all sides, hemmed in from every quarter, the outlaws left the roads and took to the fields and woods. They were in sore straits. Without a guide, for Bill Chadwell, who was to bring them safely out of the country, was lying dead in Northfield; the little band of fugitives knew not which way to turn. The country was strange, the route unknown. Still they sped onward, turning and twisting, doubling on their trail, hiding in thick bushes, making wide detours to avoid their pursuers, skirting cultivated fields and stealing past towns and villages, but always pushing on.

Jim Younger, suffering from a terrible wound, was enduring untold agonies. His blood many times served as a trail for his hunters.

They left Rice County, and passed into Le Seur County, and finally, after six days of terrible suffering, reached the vicinity of Mankato. For six days they had lived on green corn, and famished with hunger, they came to a farm house and begged for a chicken. But their pursuers were close at hand. They were seen and fired upon, and both the James brothers received serious wounds.

MURDER OF WESTFALL.

They had long ago turned their horses loose, and
were making this dreadful retreat on foot. Escaping from the men who had seen them at the farm
house, they slunk into the woods and the next day
agreed to separate. Jesse and Frank James sought
the bottoms of the Blue Earth river, and Clell
Miller, with the three Younger brothers, took
another route.

The latter party passed through Blue Earth
County, and entered Watonwau County. Here they
were seen, and Sheriff McDonald tracked them to a
swamp near Madelin, and the four bandits were
surrounded. Hundreds of men flocked to the
scene, closer and closer was the human coil
tightened around the doomed four.

Hungry and starving, covered with wounds, their
clothing torn to shreds, their shoes worn away to
the bare soles, the pitiful four, back to back,
fought four hundred. They saw there was no escape,
and with the desperation of despair, they grit
their teeth and fought. A rifle ball tore away the
lower jaw of Jim Younger, and his shriek of agony
chilled the blood of all who heard it. Yet, he
fought on.

Again an agonizing yell penetrated the dismal
recesses of the swamp, and Clell Miller sank to the
ground, and died. But still the three brothers
fought. Fought while the cordon of men drew
nearer, fought while the rifles of their pursuers
were almost touching them, fought until with a

sudden rush of many men, they were held by strong arms, and bound by stronger cords.

They were taken to Madelia, and there they lay for months, suffering from wounds which would have killed ordinary men. At last they were brought to trial before the Rice County Court, in Faribault, and, pleading "guilty", were taken to Stillwater, and the penitentiary gates closed upon them for the rest of their lives. They were doomed to a living death.

Jesse and Frank James escaped. After leaving the Younger brothers, they plunged into a wild unbroken wilderness, with no guide but the sun by day and the stars by night. Surrounded on all sides by determined foes, they were constantly in peril of detection. So closely were they pursued, that for ten days they lived on green corn and raw potatoes, not daring to make a fire. They swam rivers and waded streams, climbed hills and dove into dark gullies. But, through it all they passed safely, until the open country was reached, and here they bought horses, and secured a warm meal. All night they rode, and were congratulating themselves on their escape, when they were met by seven armed and mounted men, who attempted to arrest them. But the James boys were on horses, and armed, and when they left the attacking party, two of them were killed, and three wounded.

Through Iowa they rode and into Missouri, and it was not until they had reached Clay County, that they breathed freely, for then they were safe.

But their gang was broken up. Bill Chadwell Charlie Pitts and Clell Miller were dead. Jim, Bob, and Cole Younger were in the Stillwater prison. But the James brothers were left. The two were alone to tell the tale of that disastrous raid on the Northfield bank. Cole Younger's presentiment had been realized. It was a fatal error, an irretrievable mistake.

CHAPTER XXVII

For the next three years, Missouri was freed from
the James brothers. They found that even Clay
County would not shield them from the pursuing
fury of the Northfieldians, and making discretion
the better part of valor, the two outlaws bade
their mother a fond farewell, and journeyed to the
land of the Montezumas. It is said that they
settled in the northern part of the State of Chihua-
hua, Mexico, and in the course of several months,
secured some well filled purses from traveling
tourists and merchants.

While they were living in that country, a caravan
of six pack mules, each carrying 150 pounds of
silver, and guarded by eighteen men, was captured
by five men, the guards killed and dispersed, and
the treasure taken by the robbers. The leaders in
this little episode were said to have been Jesse
and Frank James. But this is scarcely true.
Silver bullion, such as was carried by pack mules,

was not so easily converted into coin of the
realm.

Too many inquisitive questions were asked, and
one could hardly sell it as one could old clothing
or ancient shoes. It is hardly possible that all
the highway robberies committed at this time,
could have been done by the James brothers. It
became quite the habit, when any crime of more
than ordinary atrocity was heard of, to at once lay
it to either Jesse or Frank James, or both.

Doubtless both the young brigands robbed, plundered and murdered, during these three years of
exile, but this period of their lives is shrouded
in obscurity, and romancers have taken advantage
of this indefiniteness to weave all manner of romantic tales which have the James brothers as heroes.

They have been pictured as attending fandangoes,
and, in a spirit of mere mischief inciting a row
which would enable them to display their superior
marksmanship, or their dashing qualities of
bravery, always, of course, killing something less
than a baker's dozen of Greasers, and carrying off
the most beautiful maidens present at the dance.

But the origin of these tales is clouded in mys-
tery. They only existed in the fertile brain of
some romancer.

The fact is, that it would have been positively un-
safe for the two James brothers to court any sort of
publicity. There were laws of extradition in existence which would land them into the hands of the

United States authorities, and bring a sudden termination to their career.

But writers must live and Jesse James has been
the means of paying many a board bill for some
moneyless ink-slinger.

The limit was reached though, the limit of
credulity, when the blood stained villian is credited with rescuing a fair young maiden from the
hands of a band of Greasers who had abducted the
beauteous damsel from her father's home. The
story goes that the brothers, hearing of the outrage,
shed manly tears of pity over the sad fate of the
unfortunate lady, and then, swearing the customary
oath—it is absolutely essential, in affairs of this
kind, that the gallant would-be rescuers should
grasp each others hand and swear deep and loud,
that they will not return until they bring the
abducted maiden, safe and secure, to her gray-
haired sire, they mounted their fleet chargers and
sallied forth on their noble errand of rescue.

After a forced march of many miles, they came
upon the band of woman stealers. As usual, the
band was eating and drinking, and making merry
over their exploits, and, as is also usual, the unfortunate damsel was seated apart from them, wearied,
sad, and heart-broken, attended by the ever-faithful
colored boy who always dies before he leaves his
mistress.

Then came the charge, the terrible volley, and
at once, half the Greasers were killed, and the

other half sent flying over the plains while the fair lady fainted, and was only brought around by the devoted attentions of Jesse James, and an unstinted supply of brandy.

It was all very pretty, but somewhat shopworn.

If Jesse James did do this, is was because the father of the girl offered a good sized bonus to any one that would rescue his daughter. A man who would heartlessly and without any compunctions of conscience, shoot down an unarmed man simply because he refused to give up the combination of a bank-vault, or who would deliberately cut the throat of an old, gray-haired man, merely to avenge a fancied insult, is not in the habit of going around the country rescuing maidens, unless there is something in it. Scarcely.

CHAPTER XXVIII

THREE BLISSFUL YEARS—MISSOURI'S RUDE AWAKENING
—THE GLENDALE RAID—CHICAGO AND ALTON RAIL-
ROAD HELD UP—PLUCKY WILL GRIMES—JESSE
JAMES' TELEGRAM—A THIEF TO CATCH A
THIEF—JIM ANDERSON MURDERED—
GEORGE SHEPHERD SHOOTS JESSE
JAMES — PREMATURE
JUBILATION

For three blissful years, Missouri had lived in happy security. For three years no sensational reports of another flagrant crime had been flashed over the wires, giving the outside world further opportunities of jeering and jibing or make sarcastic paragraphs in sneering journals regarding the law and order of the scourged State.

And Missouri had really begun to think that she was at last effectually and permanently rid of her "thorn in the flesh." She felt that "she could occasionally take a cat-nap once in a while," without having a robbery or murder committed.

She even dared imagine that she could now safely indulge in a good night's sleep.

But Missouri was too sanguine. Her pests were not dead, but merely sleeping, and one day, Missouri awoke herself from her sweet dream of security, with a great gasp of terror, for Jesse

James had once more shaken the land with his heavy tread.

Glendale, a station on the Kansas City branch of the Chicago and Alton R. R. is located in Lafayette County, Missouri. It is nothing but a flag-station, situated in a lonely country, rough and rugged in character, full of ravines and gullies, and surrounded by large hills. Besides the station, there was little else to the place. A general store, similar in character to most country stores, connected with the post office, and a few frame buildings, constituted the tangible part of Glendale.

On the evening of October 7th, 1879, the post master and the rest of Glendale, with the exception of the station agent, were loafing before the door of the post office when a body of rough looking men, masked and armed with revolvers and knives suddenly appeared.

Without losing any time, the citizens of Glendale were marched to the railway station, with strict orders to keep quiet tongues in their heads. .

Arriving at the station, the leader stepped inside, and approaching the agent, Mr. McIntyre, remarked casually that he wanted to send a message.

"All right," said Mr. McIntyre, coming forward "what is it?"

In a jiffy he was seized, the telegraph instrument torn from the wires and demolished, and he was told that he was a prisoner.

"Now lower that green light!" was the next command.

"But the train will stop if I do."

"Just so.   That is what we want it to do.   Come, lower that green light, or—" and the sentence was completed by a significant movement of the revolver.   Helpless to do aught else, the agent lowered the green light, as he had been ordered.

"Is there any one up stairs?" inquired the leader.

"Yes, my mother and Mr. W. E. Bridges, traveling auditor of the road." said McIntyre, telling the truth, for he could do nothing else.

One of the men assended the stairs, and before Mrs. McIntyre or Mr. Bridges was aware that anything out of the common was on the tapis, the auditor was robbed of his watch and money, and sent down stairs.

When these preliminary arrangements had been completed, the masked men concealed themselves and waited for the train.

It drew up, and stopped.   As it did so, two of the robbers sprang into the engine cab, and demanded the coal hammer.

"What do you want with it?" asked the engineer.

"Never mind! Hand it here quick or you'll never use it again."

The engineer reluctantly handed over the hammer to the determined borrower, who immediately applied it vigorously to the sturdy doors of the express car, which had been bolted at the first alarm, by the messenger, William Grimes. This plucky fellow made a bold attempt to save the treasure intrusted to his charge, and hastily taking the money from the safe, crammed it into a valise, and made a break for the rear door, but he was too late; the raiders had entered the car and their revolvers were leveled at his head.

"Here, you," demanded one of them, "give me the key of the safe, and be quick about it, too!"

"You will have to take it if you want it," was the stout-hearted answer.

A savage blow from the butt of a revolver stretched him senseless upon the floor.

In ten minutes the safe was emptied, the money taken from the bag, the valuable express packages secured, and the robbers were on their horses, flying from the scene, with $40,000 of stolen plunder.

Before leaving, however, one of the gang wrote a bravado message and told Mr. Bridges to send it to the Kansas City Journal from the next station.

The dispatch was dated from Blue Springs, and read as follows.

"We are the boys who are hard to handle, and we will make it hot for the boys who will try to take us." and was signed with the names of Jesse James, Frank James, Jack Bishop, Jim Cummings and Cool Carter.

For some time there were doubts in the minds of many, that either of the James boys were implicated in this robbery. Attempts were made by their friends to prove that neither Jesse nor Frank were within five-hundred miles of the place at the time, but subsequent developments dispelled any doubts and established beyond any arguments, that Frank James planned the raid and was present, and that Jesse James was the active leader.

Major James Liggett, of Kansas City, began active operations to run the robbers to earth. Other schemes and plans had failed, but the Major concluded that he would try again.

George Shepherd, who had been captured and sent to penitentiary for participating in the Huntington bank robbery, had served his time and come out. Before long, he was again at his old tricks, and was a member of the James gang.

It seems that Shepherd had a grievance against not only Jesse James, but Jim Anderson. A nephew of Shepherd's was found murdered and robbed of $1,000 and he accused Jesse and Jim of "doing the job."

It was through this Shepherd that Major Liggett hoped to secure Jesse and Frank James.

Getting hold of Shepherd, he so worked upon his feelings, that the ex-convict readily promised to betray the boys into the Major's hand, but Shepherd determined to take matters in his own hands.

Revenge was sweet, and he wished to taste the toothsome article.

Decoying Anderson to a lonely place, he accused him of murdering his nephew. Gaining a half admission from the outlaw, Shepherd suddenly drew his bowie knife and cut the throat of the self-convicted wretch.

Soon after, riding alone with Jesse James, the latter unsuspecting of any danger, Shepherd suddenly fired at him, and, as he believed, killed him.

Great was the excitement when the news came that the redoubtable outlaw, the famous bandit, was dead.

Great was the rejoicing over the demise of this wonderful marauder, this audacious train robber, this blood-stained murderer. His own mother believed—or claimed she did—that he was killed, and the entire state of Missouri congratulated itself that at last, her dread foe was dead—but he wasn't. The wound received from Shepherd was not mortal, although so serious he well-nigh died, but he lived; Reserved for more dark deeds; Kept for a longer career of blood and crime.

CHAPTER XXIX

A daring adventure of the Dick Turpin order, an episode of highwaymanship which ranks with the most artistic exploits of Paul Clifford, was the robbing of the Cave Coach, in September of 1880.

The Mammoth Cave of Kentucky, that wonderful catacomb of nature, is a favorite objective point for the tourists. To reach it, the majority of the curious disembarked at Cave City on the L. & N. R. R., and taking the Concord coach, journeyed to the Cave, which is some ten miles distant. The road runs through a diversified country, threading some dense patches of timber. On the evening of September 6th, 1880, seven gentlemen and one lady were passengers in the coach, which had reached a point midway between Cave City and Mammoth Cave; the party, entirely free from all apprehensions of danger, was enjoying the cool air of the September evening, and beguiling the journey by relating all the anecdotes and legends associated with that romantic region.

The coach had fairly entered a dense timber, when the security of the tourists was rudely shocked by the sudden appearance of two masked horsemen, who drove up before the coach team, and with leveled revolvers, cried:

"Halt!"

The driver, who recognized in one of the saucy strangers, the redoubtable Frank James, pulled in his horses, and warned the passengers to submit without a struggle if they valued their lives.

The coach at a stand-still, one of the horsemen rode alongside, and, in a pleasant, affable tone, remarked:

"Will you please come out of the stage?"

Without delay, the men quitted their seats, and stood before the polite and urbane outlaw.

"Now, gentlemen," continued the road agent, still preserving his civil tone, "You will greatly oblige a pair of persecuted moonshiners, who are suffering because of the unjust impositions of a greedy government, by contributing a small portion of your wealth for their benefit."

Touched by this appeal, which was rendered all the more pathetic by a careless gesture with a revolver, the gentlemen went down in their pockets, and made up a very handsome purse.

The combined efforts of the generous passengers

amounted to $950 in cash, and about $200 worth of jewelry.

After this exhibition of charity Frank James introduced himself to Miss Roundtree, the lady passenger, and in the most polite terms, begged her to convey to a certain young lady of Lebanon, the sincere expressions of his most grateful consideration.

Then turning to the amazed gentlemen, he explained to them that this was no robbery, not at all. It was simply a justifiable act on their part. They were moonshiners, engaged in a business which the harsh mandates of a discriminating government had branded as illegal. They were honest, hard-working men; but so severe had been the persecutions by the minions of the Revenue Service, that they had been forced to adopt the same business.

They were merely exacting revenue, it was a tariff for revenue only.

With this explanation, they courteously requested the passengers to resume their places in the coach, and after a cordial farewell, permitted the tourists to proceed.

Misery loves company and the depressed travelers felt better when they learned afterwards that Mr. George Croghow, one of the proprietors of Mammoth Cave, had been held up by the gentlemanly scamps, and relieved of $700.

But Frank James and Jim Cummings rode

merrily away, free of heart and full in purse, happy in the consciousness that they had performed their duty in a highly exemplary manner, in a way which was entirely above reproach; a pair of jolly slashing, saucy blades were Frank James and Jim Cummings.

CHAPTER XXX

AN ATROCIOUS CRIME—ROBBERY AND MURDER—WILLIAM
WESTFALL SHOT DOWN—MC'MILLAN SLAUGH-
TERED — PANIC-STRICKEN PASSENGERS — A
BRAVE MESSENGER—THE JAMES
BROTHERS BRUTAL
MURDERERS

From September of 1880, until July of the next
year, nothing was heard of the Jesse James brigands. The outlaws, secure in their retreats, remained unmolested and unheard. The excitement
of the Presidential election, had taken the attention of the country, and the temporary ripple caused
by the Mammoth Cave affair had calmed down.
Then came Guiteau's pistol shot, which laid low
the beloved President of the United States, Gen.
James Garfield, and the entire Republic held its
breath in heart-chilling horror. For days the
bulletins were watched with feverish anxiety by
the excited community. For days the Chief Executive lingered between death and life.

Then came the joyful news that he was gaining
strength, and comforted by the false news, the
people breathed more freely when the telegraph
wires bore to all parts, of the country, the tale of
another outrage, and the slumbering passions of

a great people leaped into a flame when they read the lurid headlines of their daily papers, which told that two more innocent lives had been sacrificed to the rapacious greed of the insatiable Jesse James and his villainous adherents.

It was on Friday evening, July 15th, 1881, that the long train on the Chicago, Rock Island & Pacific road left Kansas City. There was the usual number of passengers, but the express freight, in charge of C. H. Murray, the agent, was unusually light. There was about $2,000 in money and valuables, and a few silver bricks.

William Westfall, the ill-fated conductor, was in charge of the train. Nothing unusual occurred until Cameron was reached, where a number of men boarded the train, and again at Winston another consignment of rough fellows was taken aboard.

They had proceeded scarcely a mile from Winston when the bell cord was hastily jerked, but the fireman suspecting something was wrong shouted to the engineer not to stop, but to "give her hell." Turning his head, the engineer was terrified to find two masked men with extended revolvers, scrambling down the coal heap in the tender. With a shout of warning to his fireman, he threw the throttle forward, shutting off steam, and plunging through the window in front of his seat, ran along the foot boards amid a hail of pistol shots. With his fireman he clung to the pilot until the engine slowed down, and then escaped to the woods.

In the meantime, murder was done in the train. Westfall, the conductor, was collecting tickets, when a masked man, dressed in a long linen duster followed by other men similarly attired, entered the car. Rushing up to the conductor, one of the ruffians mumbled something to the effect that he was the man he wanted, and immediately leveling the pistol, shot the conductor through the head. Not satisfied, he fired again and again at the fallen man, who was flooding the floor of the car with his life-blood.

A stone-mason, employed by the railroad company, McMillan by name, entered the car at the same time and was immediately shot dead by one of the masked murderers. Then arose a scene of tumult and confusion. The panic-stricken passengers were beside themselves with fear. Crawling under the seats, slinking into the corners of their berths, sinking to the floor, they huddled together in abject terror, trembling with fear.

But the marauders made no attempt to rob the passengers, although many of them, in pitiful dread of their life, voluntarily offered their money and watches. The robbers seemed bent on doing but one thing. That is, terrorizing the passengers.

The real work was going on in the baggage car.

The express messenger C. H. Murray, and the baggage man, Stampe, were together in the car, the door partly open for ventilating purposes, as the night was warm.

The sudden stoppage of the train, brought Stampe to the door to see what was the matter.

He was suddenly grasped by four masked men, who cried, in threatening tones:

"Come out, you—of a—! Come out."

The baggage man was hauled out of the car, and was threatened with instant death if he stirred a muscle.

Murray, alarmed by these movements, slammed and locked the door, and hastily constructed a barricade of trunks, behind which he crouched.

Finding the door locked, the bandits began firing through it, one of the bullets grazing Murray's shoulder. Enraged and furious, at being thus balked, the robbers proceeded to smash in the door with an ax and finally bursting it, rushed into the car.

"Where is that — — — —?" yelled one.

"Here I am." replied Murray rising from his hiding place. "What do you want?"

In an instant he was grasped, and flung to the ground and the key of the safe demanded. The demand was emphasized by a blow from the butt of a pistol.

Holding a revolver to his head, they opened the safe, and took all the money. Great was their disappointment when they found so small a booty.

Believing Murray had secreted the greater portion of it, they asked him how much money was aboard. Murray replied that he did not know.

"Then you ought to know." said the leader.
"What in hell are you in charge for if you don't
know? Come tell me quick, or I'll kill you."

"You've got everything but those silver bricks."
was the cool response.

"Oh! d—n your bricks." was the disgusted re-
joinder.

Satisfied that they had all there was, they struck
him again with the revolver, and left the car.

They had only secured $2,000, but they had com-
mitted a cruel and atrocious double murder. Leaving the dead and living, the plundered car, and
the terrified passengers, the masked men disappeared in the woods, and rode away.

It did not seem their policy to rob the passengers,
for not a cent was taken from the cars. They
meant to rob the express alone.

The killing of Westfall was a heinous crime of the
most flagrant character. He had not said a word;
yet he was shot down without mercy.

The presumption is that the James brothers paid
off an old score in killing him. He had aroused
their enmity somehow, and this was their revenge.
It was a cruel, brutal, cowardly act, and aroused a
storm of indignation never before created.

CHAPTER XXXI

GLENDALE AGAIN—THE BLUE-CUT AFFAIR—BREAKING
OPEN EXPRESS CARS—ARGUMENT BY REVOLVERS—
PLUCKY ACTION OF HAZELBAKER, THE CON-
DUCTOR—FLAGGING A TRAIN UNDER DIF-
FICULTIES—CHAPPY FOOTE TREATED
BY JESSE JAMES—A BOMBAS-
TIC TIRADE

Beyond any doubt, the men engaged in this last raid, were Jesse and Frank James, Pope Wells, Jim Cummings, Miller, Palmer, and young Samuels, brother-in-law to Jesse. This is the opinion of Mr. M. A. Lowe the attorney of the railroad, and sheriff Crosby of Daviess County.

Mr. William Pinkerton stated that the robbery and murder was undoubtedly the work of the James gang, and the testimony of the passengers aboard the ill-fated train all tend to this conclusion.

Again came up the much-discussed question "Cannot something be done to rid Missouri of this lawless band of robbers and murderers?"

Again and again were bountiful rewards offered for the apprehension, conviction, detection, or death of the bandits. Again were strong parties organized for pursuit, and again did it all end in nothing. For several months this agitation was continued and while the interest was still una-bated, while the police were still making strenuous efforts to do something, another train was held up by the same band of train robbers.

Again was the Chicago & Alton R. R. the victim and the robbery occurred near Glendale, where two years previous, Jesse James had taken $40,000 from the passengers and express company.

It was September 7th, 1881, about 9 o'clock in the evening, when the train was brought to a stand still in a deep cut where the Missouri Pacific crosses the Alton tracks. The sudden stop was caused by a huge pile of broken stone, which was across the track. Immediately a dozen masked men dashed into the cars, while the leader, approaching the engine, said to Foote, the engineer:

"Step down out of that engine and do as I tell you, or I'll kill you!"

Foote, after some parleying, did so, and at the same time brought down the coal pick at the command of the armed outlaw.

With his fireman, he was marched to the express car, and ordered to break the door down. This he did.

Fox the express messenger, anticipating trouble, had secreted himself in the grass near the track, and only came out when the leader threatened to kill the engineer and fireman unless the messenger showed up.

With menacing revolvers they compelled Fox to open the safe, giving him several raps on the head with the butts of their revolvers to accelerate his

movements. Cramming the money—some $2,500
into a leather bag they carried, they left a guard
over the engineer, fireman and messenger and went
back into the train.

While these exciting events were taking place
around the engine and baggage car, others of the gang
were passing and repassing through the passenger
coaches, firing their revolvers into the roof of the
car, swaggering and bullying, declaring with deep
oaths and obscene remarks, that they were going
to hold up every passenger on the train. The conductor, Mr. Hazelbaker, and the brakeman, Mr.
Burton, comprehending the condition of affairs at
the first alarm, begged the passengers to be sub-
missive, and warned them that resistance to the
robbers meant death. This duty done, the two
brave men made instant preparations to flag a
freight train following them. In doing this, they
performed as courageous an act as was ever recorded, for, as with a red lantern in hand, the two
heroic train men leaped from the rear platform,
they were greeted with a volley of bullets, and the
robbers kept up an incessant fire as long as they
were in range.

The danger of telescoping over, for Burton remained with the red lantern to flag the train,
Hazelbaker returned to his charge, and seating
himself waited quietly to be robbed.

The leader of the band, a tall, athletic man,

shoved his revolver under the conductor's nose and said:

"D—n you; that is the pistol that killed West-fall at Winston. You tell your G—d d—d company that Jesse James told you so."

In due time the robbers went through the train, robbing every passenger, securing in all, with the express money, about $15,000.

Their work finished the robbers suddenly disappeared, and were quickly lost to sight in the dense shadow of the night.

Before leaving however, the leader of the gang came to Foote, the engineer, and said:

"Chappy Foote, you'r a d—d fine fellow to run on the road. Here's $2. Get a drink in the morning, and drink it for Jesse James. You want to get off the road though, or you'll get killed. We are going to bust this road and the Rock Island too, d—n them. They are offering too many rewards. We've no grudge against Pullman. He's white, and don't offer any rewards. We'll switch off the Pullmans and burn the rest. I am the man who killed Westfall at Winston. He was too fresh and drew a gun."

This tirade was unlike Jesse James. He was not given to brag but rather the other thing, yet, Jesse James led that raid.

CHAPTER XXXII.

The Blue Cut robbery, as narrated in the last chapter, marked the turning point of the long lane of Jesse James' career. Gov. Crittenden, of Missouri, had taken hold of the outlaw matter, and was pushing it with great energy. He had resolved, fair means or foul, to sweep this murderous gang of cut-throats from the face of the earth, and bent his energies to the work in a way which was bound to win.

Gathering together the proper officials of the various railroads and express companies that had suffered by the hands of Jesse James, and his associate desperadoes, he put the case to them squarely and explicitly. He told them he wanted to offer a reward of $50,000 for Jesse and Frank James, dead or alive. He said that he felt warranted in offering such an immense pecuniary inducement.

DEATH OF JESSE JAMES.

The railroads and express companies gladly and willingly pledged their financial support, and the rewards were offered $10,000 for either Frank or Jesse James dead or alive, and $5,000 for each member of their gang, dead or alive.

With this mighty lever in his hand, the Governor set to work to move the proper machinery by which he hoped to accomplish his object.

He felt that the honor among thieves was a quality of honor which would not stand against the pressure of ten thousand tempting dollars.

He knew that the natural cupidity of such men as composed the James gang would be excited by the princely rewards, and that sooner or later, he would have the pleasure of drawing a check for $10,000 in exchange for the live or dead body of one or both the notorious outlaws.

But the two men, most active and more directly responsible for the complete annihilation of the Jesse James band were Sheriff John R. Timberlake of Clay County, and H. H. Craig, Police Commissioner of Kansas City.

On the 16th, of February 1882, a veiled woman called on Gov. Crittenden, at his office in Jefferson City, and inquired upon what terms an outlaw could surrender to the authorities. The Governor replied that it was altogether a matter of the man, who he was. If it was Jesse or Frank James he would promise no immunity from punishment, but if any other minor member of the gang came in, with the honest intention of abandoning his former life, and having a sincere desire to live a better life, he would be assured of protection, especially so, continued the crafty executive, if he would promise to faithfully assist the officers of the law in capturing the James brothers

After their interview, the mysterious woman left, and three days later, Dick Little, a trusted member of Jesse James' company, surrendered to Sheriff Timberlake. This was on February 19th.

On the 22d, he was conveyed to Jefferson City, where he made a volumnious confession.

This was not the beginning of the plot, however, which was to end the career of Jesse James.

The outlaw had moved to St. Joseph, Missouri, the preceding November, where he lived quietly under the name of Thomas Howard, with his wife and two children. With him came a young man known as Robert Johnson, but whose name was really Robert Ford.

He was a cousin of Jesse, and possessed his entire confidence. But the cousin was a false friend. He was a traitor in the camp, a veritable serpent in the grass, waiting but for a favorable opportunity to strike, treacherous, despicable and false hearted, this Robert Ford was nothing more nor less than a detective employed by the authorities to capture or kill Jesse James, the man who took him to his home and fireside, sheltered him, and

Jesse James and his Band 12

clothed him. This Ford was employed by Gov. Crittenden, Sheriff Timberlake and Mr. Craig. He was joined by his brother Charlie, Sunday, March 26th. The latter, who was also in the plot against Jesse James, was invited by the outlaw to visit him for the purpose of perfecting a plan to rob the bank at Platte City. Funds were getting low, and it was proposed to draw upon the exchequer of the Platte City Bank.

The Burgess murder trial was fixed for April 4th, and was to be held in Platte City. Jesse James was to first make a careful examination of the premises, and then when the attention of the town was taken up by the trial, to make a bold dash, and rob the bank.

The Ford boys approved of the scheme, and entered enthusiastically into the affair.

The preparations completed, the outlaw remained at home waiting for the appointed day, little dreaming that he would never again mount his horse and dash into a terror stricken town as of yore. His days were numbered upon the fingers of his hand, but unconscious of the fate which was to overwhelm him in so short a time, the confident bank robber spent his last days on earth scheming and planning new raids, concocting new deviltries and devising means for acquiring fresh plunder.

CHAPTER XXXIII

Monday April 3rd, 1882, was an eventful day for St. Joseph, Mo. A shot was fired that morning, between eight and nine o'clock, by a smooth-faced boy of twenty years, which did more than all the Pinkertons, United States Service, Missouri detectives, sheriffs, marshals and constables had been able to do in ten years; a mere lad, not old enough to vote, had dared do a deed which would have caused many a stout heart to turn coward, and make many a brave man tremble to even dream of.

This Monday morning, April 3rd, 1882, a bullet was sped which forever stilled the heart of the most famous outlaw the world has ever seen—Jesse James!

Jesse James was shot by Robert Ford, and died almost immediately.

For months, the Ford boys had watched for a

favorable opportunity to kill the intrepid bandit. On this morning after breakfast, Jesse and Charlie Ford went to the stable to curry the horses, and get everything ready for the Platte City bank raid. The day was unusually warm, and they returned to the house, Jesse remarking: "It's an awfully hot day," pulled off his coat and vest, and tossed them on the bed.

Robert Ford was in the room at the time, and a significant glance passed between himself and his brother, when Jesse unbuckled his belt, and said:

"I guess I'll take off my pistols for fear somebody will see them if I walk in the yard."

So saying, he placed the belt, in which he carried two revolvers—45 calibre, one Smith & Wesson and the other, a Colt, upon the bed with his coat and vest.

He then picked up a dusting brush, and stepping on a chair, commenced dusting a picture.

His back was turned to the brothers, his pistols were out of reach, they were alone in the room, and the time had come.

Silently, the Ford boys stepped in between Jesse and the bed, and, at a motion from Charlie, both drew their guns; Robert, quick as a flash, raised his weapon, and glanced along the barrel; as he did so, Jesse made a movement as if to turn his head, but there was a nervous pressure on the trigger, a sharp report, and the 45 calibre lead ball crashed its deadly way through Jesse James' head, entering at the base of the brain and crashing out through the forehead.

Not a word was said, not a sound but the report of Robert Ford's pistol; there was a tottering, swaying of the athletic figure on the chair, a sudden relaxing of muscles, a quiver, and then the king of the outlaws fell heavily to the floor, and gasped out his life with the crimson blood streaming from the awful wound in his forehead.

Mrs. James was in the kitchen at the time, but hearing the shot, rushed into the fatal room. On the floor, she saw the body of her husband, and running to the rear fence were his murderers, pistols in hand.

"Robert," she screamed, "You have done this! Come back!"

"I swear to God I did not." was the reply.

Dropping on her knees, she raised her husband's head in her arms. He was still breathing, and when she asked him if he was hurt, he endeavored to speak, but could not. It did not last long. A few more gasps, a last sigh, and Jesse James died in his wife's arms.

Charlie Ford explained to Mrs. James, that a pistol had gone off accidentally.

"Yes," said Mrs. James. "I guess it went off on purpose." She was wonderfully calm, was this slender, fair woman. But for years she had lived in daily expectancy of just such a scene, and had schooled herself to bear it stoically when it came.

Anxious to get away from the home to which they had brought such dire desolation, the two boys left the house, and telegraphed the news to Gov. Crittenden and Sheriff Timberlake, then proceeded to Marshall Craig's office to give themselves in custody. They were told that the marshall with a posse of officers had already started to the Harwood house, as news of the tragedy had reached him.

Even Craig, although he knew the Ford boys were after Jesse James, never suspected that Howard and James were the same person. Hurrying back, the Ford brothers gave themselves up to Craig, telling him that the man they had killed was Jesse James, and they claimed the reward.

When Marshall Craig heard that the dead man was Jesse James, he exclaimed:

"My God! do you mean to tell me this is Jesse James?"

"Yes, that is Jesse Jmaes." was the proud response. "We have killed him and we don't deny it. We feel proud that we have killed a man who is known all over the world as the most notorious desperado that ever lived."

They were then taken back to the police station, and securely guarded.

Sheriff Timberlake had telegraphed to the Ford brothers to stay where they were, and he would come at once.

The news spread like wild-fire, and St. Joseph

never witnessed such intense excitement. The streets were thronged with a crowd of agitated citizens, who could scarcely comprehend the fact that Jesse James, the terrible, murderous outlaw, who had kept Missouri in a state of terror for years, had lived for months among them, and was now lying dead in his home. The body had been removed to the morgue, and the place was beseiged by hundreds of curious people, anxious to see the remains of the terrible man of whom they had heard so much. But they were obliged to curb their morbid curiosity for a time, as Coroner Heddens refused admittance to any except representatives of the press, and the proper officials.

The coroner's jury was impaneled, and after viewing the remains, adjourned to the old circuit court rooms, where the inquest was to be held.

The jury consisted of W. H. Chooning, J. W. Moore, Warren Samuels, Thomas Morris, William Turner and William George. The chief witnesses were Mrs. James, Charles and Robert Ford and James Little, who had been brought from Jefferson City for that purpose.

Many people refused to believe that the dead man was Jesse James. Some sneered and with the cynicism of deferred hope, expressed the opinion that Jesse James was as much alive now as he ever was. When Robert Ford was told that many people believed that Jesse James was still living, he became indignant.

"So they say the dead man is some one else, do they? Then they are mistaken. I met Jesse James three years ago, and I am not mistaken now. He moved here to St. Joseph last November, and assumed the name of Thomas Howard. He rented a house on the corner of Lafayette street and Twenty-first, and after staying there two months, secured the house No. 1318 Lafayette street, and paid $14.00 a month rent. My brother, Charlie, and I know nearly all his gang, but have never worked with them.

I was in with the detectives, and was with the party that arrested Clarance Hite, in Kenutcky, last February. He got twenty-five years in the penitentiary.

Jesse James never suspected either Charlie or myself, and as his gang was all busted up, he wanted to make us members. He went to Kearney, to see his mother two weeks ago, and when he came back, we told him we wanted to join his band, and he said "All right."   Charlie came here a week ago Sunday and I followed last Sunday night, and we put up at his house.

We have been watching for a chance to do him up for months, but he was always on the lookout, and we knew that if we failed, it was all up with us. He kept close to the house during the day-time, but in the evening, he would go down town and get his papers; the Chicago Tribune, Cincinnati Commercial, and Kansas City Times, regularly.

He kept himself posted on what was going on all over the world.

Gov. Crittenden had offered a reward for Jesse James, dead or alive, and we were after that reward. But we could get no chance until this morning. He was in the front room where he slept and did the most careless thing of his life. He took off his coat and vest and laid his pistols on the bed, then stepped on a chair to dust a picture. As he did so, we got between him and his guns and drew on him. I was eight feet away, and when he heard my pistol cock, he turned like lightning, but I pulled, and he fell at Charlie's feet.

Not one of us spoke a word. We got our hats and went to the telegraph office, and telegraphed what we had done to Gov. Crittenden, Captain Craig of Kansas City, and Sheriff Timberlake of Clay County. The sheriff replied: "I will come at once. Stay there until I come."

"That is Jesse James, and we killed him."

The newspapers, the next day, published the most sensational reports of the murder, for murder it was, although it vindicated the law.

The startling news was received with considerable joy by the Pinkerton's in Chicago, and William Pinkerton especially was well pleased, remarking:

"Good! Then John Wicher is avenged at last."

Hundreds of people flocked into St. Joseph, that wanted to get a vision of the dead man, and the town was in a great commotion until after the funeral.

The sentiments regarding the act, were as varied as the people who expressed them. Some thought the killing a contemptible, despicable assassination, not recognizing the great truth that "the end justified the means."

Others, while they regarded the killing as a justifiable and legal man-slaughter, by which the majesty of the law was upheld, were inclined to cast approbrium upon the underhand method employed, while there were others who lauded the Ford brothers to the skies, making heroes of them, and praising their bravey in thus killing such a well-known desperado.

Mrs. Samuels, who received the news by telegraph from Mrs. James, bore the shock with the stoicism characteristic of the stern-visaged woman.

She shed no tears, nor indulged in any outward demonstations of sorrow, but a baneful gleam shot from her hard eyes, when she read that Bob Ford had killed her son, and Dick Little had placed a criminating and detailed confession in the hands of the authorities. Hastening to St. Joseph, she sought her widowed daughter-in-law, and the meeting was pathetic in the extreme. Even then Mrs. James and Mrs. Samuels retained their unnatural composure, but, when they were permitted to see the body of the dead son and husband, their calmness forsook them, and they clung to each other with the strong embrace of sorrow and grief.

Mrs. Samuels nearly swooned when she first saw her dead son's face, and sobbed aloud.

"My poor boy! My dear son! My darling boy!"

Alone before their dead, the stricken women moaned in the agony of their dreadful loss, and gave way to unrestrained sobs of acute anguish. From the undertaker's establishment, they were driven to the court rooms to give their testimony at the inquest.

CHAPTER XXXIV

THE INQUEST—THE CROWDED COURT-ROOM—TESTIMONY
OF OFFICIALS—DICK LITTLE BEFORE THE JURY—
"WOULD TO GOD IT WERE NOT"—THE FORD
BOYS CHARGED WITH MURDER—"TRAITOR!
TRAITOR! TRAITOR!"—THE FUNERAL
OF JESSE JAMES—COMMENTS OF
THE PRESS

The great interest created by the assassination of Jesse James was manifested by the throng that packed the court room to suffocation. Hundreds of other disappointed persons, unable to obtain admission, filled the hall and entrances, and crowded outside the building, discussing the tragic event.

H. H. Craig, Police Commissioner of Kansas City, was the first witness sworn.

He testified that the body corresponded with the description of Jesse James, and gave a detailed description. He was acquainted with both the Ford boys, and stated that Bob Ford assisted Sheriff Timberlake and himself. He was not formally commissioned, however. Robert Ford acted through his instructions, but Charles Ford did not.

Sheriff Timberlake, the next witness, said that he was acquainted with Jesse James, and recognized the body. They were personally acquainted with each other. He stated that he saw Jesse James in 1870, and knew his face. He told Robert Ford, who was employed to assist him, to get his brother Charles as a helper.

Dick Little was then sworn. He recognized the body and swore it was that of Jesse James. He was sure of it. In general appearance the body resembled Jesse James. The outlaw had a finger off his hand; so did the corpse. He recognized the scars in the thigh and side, and identified the body as that of Jesse Jame

James Finley, the next witness, testified as follows

"I am not acquainted with Jesse James. I went to the house after the shooting, and found two horses. I sent two officers after the Johnsons, as they were then called. Ford came and acknowledged the shooting. He described the wounds on the body and claimed the man was Jesse James. Ford told me there were watches and jewelry in the house. I found watches, jewelry, pistols, cartridges and a purse. I gave the purse to Mrs. James. It had some small change in it. A scarf pin was found with the marks 'J. W. J.'"

When Mrs. Samuels, the mother of Jesse James, was called, all eyes were turned upon her. Men stood in their seats, and crowded forward in their anxiety to catch a view of the now famous old woman. She walked slowly and with bowed head, to the witness stand. Although her face was stern, it had a kindly look, and her bright eyes and prominent nose gave a note-worthy appearance to her visage. She was simply and quietly dressed in black.

She testified that she was the mother of Jesse James and that she had seen his body but a moment ago.

"Is that the body of your son?" inquired the coroner.

"It is." was the answer; and then followed sobs. "Would to God it were not. And these are his orphan children," she continued, placing her hands on the heads of the son and daughter of the dead desperado. Again the old lady was moved to tears.

Requesting Mrs. James to raise her veil, the coroner asked Mrs. Samuels if she recognized her.

"Yes, she is the widow of Jesse James."

Mrs. James testified that she recognized the preceding witness as Mrs. Samuels and then the bereaved mother left the court-room.

The jury retired, and, in a short time, brought in the following verdict:

"We, the jury, find that the deceased is Jesse James, and that he came to his death by a pistol shot in the hands of Robert Ford."

Immediately afterwards, the Ford boys were committed to jail, charged with the murder of Jesse James, on a warrant sworn out by his widow.

As she was returning from the court-room, Mrs. Samuels met Dick Little, and a highly dramatic scene was enacted. With her eyes flashing passion, and her frame quivering with excitement, she sprang toward the traitor with the ferocity of a tiger.

"Traitor! Traitor! Traitor!" she exclaimed, her voice vibrating with anger. "God will send his vengeance on you for this. Oh, you villain! I would rather be in my boy's place than in yours."

The outlaw shrunk from the female fury, in abject fear.

"I did not hunt him," he pleaded. "I thought you knew who killed him?"

"Oh! God! My poor boy" was the piteous ejeculation of the gray-haired woman, as she turned away.

That night, the wife, mother and sister slept in the cottage where Jesse James had been killed, and the next day, the body was taken to Kearney, for burial.

The following is an extract from the Kansas City Times of April 6th, 1882.

St. Joseph, Mo., April 5.—Craig and Timberlake, the men who engineered Jesse's capture, have been delayed and obstructed all day by the St. Joseph officials, through jealousy. The special train has been waiting since 10 a. m., to take the body, but the city marshal would not give it up. The body was secured at 6 p. m., and taken quietly

to the depot, where the sheriff's party next prepared it to go out on the regular train to Cameron.

From there they go by a special to Kearney.
Jesse's widow, children and mother accompany the
remains. They are very nervous. The body is in
a $500 coffin furnished by Craig and Timberlake.
The funeral takes place to-morrow.

CAMERON, Mo., April 5.—Although kept very
quiet, a perfect mob was at the depot in St.
Joseph, to see the party off. The Times correspon-
dent's instructions from Timberlake, were: "Meet
us at the depot; I'll be there with the corpse."

Just as the train pulled into the depot, two car-
riages and a wagon with the coffin came up. Mrs.
Samuels stepped out of the first carriage, and lean-
ing on an officer's arm, walked into the depot, followed by a gaping crowd. Mrs. Samuels said as
she left the carriage: "Take me to the corpse; I
want to see it on board." The carriage with Mrs.
James drove back to the hotel, and the old lady
went to the baggage-car and saw the body on the
train. Timberlake and his party sat in the baggage-car to guard the body. Mrs. Samuels entered
her car and guards were placed at the doors. The
train was held for Mrs. James to come. She drove
up to the depot at a rapid pace, and, alighting, was
escorted to her seat. The crowd was thicker than
ever when the train left. Mrs. James was accompanied by Luther James, a cousin of Jesse's, from
Kansas City, her two children and Mrs. Samuels.

The train was heavily guarded. While in the
depot at St. Joseph, a short, thick-set man tried to
pull a pistol on Mrs. Samuels, but was promptly
fired out of the door and landed in the street. He
was shot at, but not hit.

At all the stations along the road, crowds gathered, anxious to see the body, the family, the officers,
or anything, and great excitement prevailed. We
arrived at Cameron at 9: 11. p. m., and were met by
an immense crowd. The ladies were taken to a
private room at the depot while waiting for the
special train, and the body was taken from the
baggage car, followed by a mob, who stood around
the windows, eager to catch a glimpse of the pine
box that covered the coffin. Mrs. Samuels and
Mrs. James are very much worn out. A dispatch
received here by Mrs. Samuels, says her youngest
son is dying at home. Thus far there have been no
signs of any outbreak or disturbance, although,
several hard characters appeared on the train. Dick
Little will not go to the funeral, but remains at
liberty. A difficulty was met here in getting a train
to Kearney, and we will probably stay here all
night.

It has been decided at last, to go to Kearney tonight. The party could not get a special train over
the Hannibal. One was kept standing all day by
that road for the party, but, thinking they had
abandoned coming, it was ordered away. W. R.
Woodland, general superintendent, telegraphed that

13

it was impossible to send a train till morning, as
the engines were all working. The Rock Island furnished a special to leave here at midnight. The
funeral takes place to-morrow, from the Baptist
church, in Kearney. The sermon will be preached
by Rev. Martin. Mrs. Samuels is afraid that the
body will be stolen. A relative stands guard on
the box all the time. The crowd here desired that
the .body be shown, but Mrs. Samuels objected,
and the box was not opened. Mrs. Samuels desired
President Rothwell, of Liberty, to speak at the
funeral. He will probably be there. Mrs. Samuels
desires Preacher Williams to preach the funeral
sermon but don't know where to find him. Williams baptized Jesse just after the war.

St. Joseph, Mo., April 5.—The body of Jesse
James was shipped from this city on the 7 o'clock
train of the Hannibal & St. Jo. Railroad this evening, in custody of Marshall Craig, of this city, and
the family of the dead desperado, consisting of L.
W. James, cousin of Jesse; R. T. Mimms, the
widow's brother, Mrs. James, Mrs. Samuels, and
the two children. It will be taken to Kearney,
Clay County, and buried on the James homestead
to-morrow. There has been considerable of a
wrangle over the remains, between H. H. Craig,
the police commissioner of Kansas City, Sheriff
Timberlake, of Clay County, and the local authorities, who insisted upon seeing the body placed in
the keeping of the relatives instead of being sent

to Kansas City. The body was officially turned
over to Mrs. James, by Coroner Heddens, this afternoon, on an order from the grand jury of Buchanan
County and the dispatch of Gov. Crittenden. The
jam on the depot platform this evening as the relatives stepped from their conveyances to take the
train was tremendous. Mrs. Samuels was the most
conspicuous personage in the throng. She insisted on having an official report from the train at
Kansas City. The commission sent up by Gov.
Crittenden, including Mattie Collens, Dick Little's
wife, arrived at a late hour last night, viewed the
remains, and identified them as those of Jesse
James. The Ford boys are close prisoners at the
county jail, and when interviewed this morning,
they betrayed a nervous anxiety about their fate.
Up to within twelve hours ago they did not seem to
realize the gravity of their situation, but to-day
Robert confessed to a reporter that if he had known
that he would have been thrown into a dingy cell
he would not have killed Jesse. The arms and
jewelry found in the outlaw's home are in the
hands of the police, who refused to surrender them
until the question of their ownership has been fully
determined. The household goods will be sold to
the highest bidder.

From the Chicago *Times*, April 4, 1882.

The killing of Jesse James rids the country of
one of the boldest and most dangerous land-pirates
who ever made war on society. He and his gang

may have not done all the iniquity that is credited
to them; their reputation doubtless led people to
attribute to them some deeds done by others.   But
no crime has ever been laid at their door that they
would not have cheerfully committed had they had
the chance.   The James brothers and the Younger
brothers have given many localities in the state of
Missouri a reputation that casts Hounslow Heath
in the shade; and Gadshill and Blue Cut, and
some other equally famous localities will not soon
be forgotten by so much of the public as ever had
occasion to travel in the state of Missouri.   The
introduction of the railway system did more than
inaugurate a new method of transportation; it
introduced several new professions, and not the
least notable of these is that of the train-robber.
The world was familiar with stage-coach robberies
at the time the railroad was inaugurated.   In a
secluded region, it was not a difficult matter to
induce the driver of a stage to halt and the passengers to divest themselves of their watches and money
But the railway train appeared to be a contrivance
for travel that the highwayman could not deal with.
The driver of a locomotive might disregard with
impunity, the summons of the masked gentlemen,
and a train of cars could certainly make better
time than even the horse whose fleetness enabled
Dick Turpin to prove an alibi.   For a while, the
road-agents, as they were euphemistically called,
looked with dismay on the substitution of steam

for horse-flesh, as a motive power, but in the course
of time, they learned that a railway train could be
robbed as easily as a stage-coach.   The robbers had
only to obstruct the track in a desolate locality, or
to embark in the train as passengers, and rob the
occupants of the cars *en route*, then compel the
engineer to stop and let them off at some convenient place not down on the schedule as even so
much as a flag-station, and the whole thing could
be done with neatness and dispatch, and also with
entire success.   In fact, the facility with which
the artists in this line of business have done their
work, creates some surprise that more brigands
were not drawn into the profession of train-robbing.
Though the thing has been essayed once or twice
elsewhere, it was confined as a regular business to
the state of Missouri, and there was growing up in
the country at large a conviction that no small
part of the population of Missouri must be in league
with the train-robbers.   It certainly does look as
though the local authorities were not as efficient as
they might have been, in the detection of the
rascals, but it must be remembered that the train-
robbers were numerous, or were believed to be so,
and they had no scruples about making themselves
disagreeable to persons who seemed unfriendly.
No man cared to make himself the target for the
rifles of the James brothers, or to invite the destruction of his house and barn, by refusing them
shelter, or giving information of their whereabouts

to the officers of the law. And so Jesse James was able to live in St. Joseph all winter, and might have been robbing another train last night, had he not, in a moment of weakness, indulged in the ceremonies of ablution. Any person who has tried it, knows how inconvenient it is to take a bath with a half a dozen large revolvers buckled around his waist. The late Mr. James was incautious enough to lay aside his choice collection of firearms. That was the moment that two spies had long been looking for. It was not attempted to arrest him. Mr. James was believed to have stated that he would not be taken alive, and the belief was universal in Missouri that he would have to be reduced to the condition of a corpse before it would be practicable to serve a warrant on him. No experiments were tried. One of the detectives, whom he supposed to be his apprentice, crept up behind him, and put a bullet in his brain. Jesse James was effectually arrested. The end was in perfect accord with his career, and he would undoubtedly have preferred dying as he did to being hanged, and the traveling public feels a good deal safer now than it would if Jesse James was merely in jail, awaiting trial. Ford's method of arrest was a little irregular, but his reputation was such, that no man could have been expected to attempt his arrest by any other means than the revolver.

CHAPTER XXXV

Charles and Robert Ford were arraigned before
Judge Sherman at St. Joseph on Monday, the 17th
of April, and both prisoners pleaded guilty to the
indictment, unhesitatingly and promptly.

No attempt was made by them to enter a defense.
They acknowledged the killing and pleaded
"guilty" in a most unconcerned manner.

Recovering from the surprise excited by the
nonchalance of the prisoners, Judge Sherman asked
them if they had anything to say why sentence
should not be passed upon them.

"Nothing," was the unconcerned reply.

The Judge then passed sentence of death upon
them, fixing the date when they were to be hanged,
at May 9th, 1882.

On the morning of the 18th of April, an uncon-
ditional pardon was granted both the Ford boys

by Gov. Thomas T. Crittenden, and Sheriff Thomas at once liberated them, but Robert's liberty was cut short, and he became very much agitated when Sheriff Trigg of Bay County, placed his hands on his shoulders, and said:

"You are my prisoner," and arrested him for complicity in the murder of Wood Hite, whose body was found a week previous in an old well on the Ford farm.

Charlie Ford went free.

After the trial of the Ford brothers, Jesse James' armory was handed over to Mrs. James. The value of the guns, weapons and knives exceeded $700.

On the 5th of October, 1882, Frank James entered the office of Gov. Crittenden, in Jefferson City.

Walking up to the governor, he surrendered himself, and unbuckling his pistol belt, laid it and the revolvers on the table, remarking:

"No living man but me has had his hands on these revolvers since 1861.

This bit of drama was the culmination of a correspondence between Frank James and the Governor.

The outlaw, tired and weary of his passionate life, rapidly nearing the grave, hurried on by the dread consumption; anxious to end his days free from apprehension of arrest or a violent death, voluntarily gave himself up. He was taken to Independence the next day and delivered into the proper hands, to await his trial.

Sentenced for life, he was afterwards pardoned out, as the deadly consumption was claiming him for a victim, and mercy tempted justice, so that he could end his days with his family.

The Jesse James band of outlaws is no more. The desperadoes are scattered, death has claimed many, the prison guards many more, and the few that remain are cautioned to depart from their wickedness, and live law-abiding lives.

On a monument of red granite, which rears its shaft fourteen feet above the grave is chiseled the following inscription:

My Husband—Our Father.

JESSE JAMES.

DIED

April 2.—1882.

Age,

34 years, 6 months, 8 days.

COLE YOUNGER'S TRIBUTE

When Cole Younger was told by one of the assistant wardens of the Stillwater Penitentiary, that Jesse James had been shot and killed, he was very much affected. After a few moment's reflection he voiced the following remarkable panegyric over the death of his old leader:

"So he is dead! Dead by the pistol! He died with his boots on. It is what he wished for. It is the death he would have chosen, though not by a traitor's hand.

"Jesse James was a brave man, he had no acquaintance with fear, and did not know the meaning of the word afraid. To his friends he was loyalty itself. In their cause he held his life as nothing. The bravest, boldest deeds of his life were performed for friendship's sake. He was the first to lead into danger, and the last to leave. Jesse James was a white man and clear grit, and never went back on his friends. But to his foes he was Satan himself. Fair means or foul, he arrived at his revenge. No danger was too great, no hardship too severe, and no place too sacred for him when after one whom he regarded as an enemy. Toward such he was merciless, cruel, treacherous, and crafty; for days or months or years, he would wait or follow, but never forgiving or forgetting, he would bide his time, and when that time came he struck, and when he struck, he killed.

"He was a wonderful man, was Jesse James, and the boys who made up his gang would lay down their lives for him. There was something about him that inspired the blindest fealty. He was a born commander, a genius in controlling men. When we were with Quantrell, there was always a struggle to get into Jesse's squad, and he was but a lad. But, young as he was, he could shoot, ride and fight better than any man in the command, and he was always successful.

"He loved his family, and they idolized him. Many a time has he ridden over a hundred miles through the enemy's lines, surrounded on all sides by Union troops, who were on the lookout for any of Quantrell's gray-coats, just to have an hour's chat with his mother. After he was married, he would spend whole weeks at his home, playing with his children, happy as a lord. But in spite of all that, he was a terrible man, and now he is dead. He was bound to be killed that way, for he was too bold—so bold that he was careless. It is a shame that he was killed by one of his own men. He wanted to be shot to death, but not by the traitor's hand. It's too bad."

www.ingramcontent.com/pod-product-compliance
Lightning Source LLC
Chambersburg PA
CBHW030830270326
41928CB00007B/978